NAOMI: A WOMAN TO FOLLOW

Naomi:
A Woman To Follow

EILEEN WALLIS

KINGSWAY PUBLICATIONS
EASTBOURNE

First published 1991

Front cover design by Vic Mitchell

British Library Cataloguing in Publication Data

Wallis, Eileen
  Naomi: a woman to follow
  1. Christianity. Scriptures. Characters
  I. Title
  222.35092

  ISBN 0–86065–900–3

Printed in Great Britain for
KINGSWAY PUBLICATIONS LTD
1 St Anne's Road, Eastbourne, E Sussex BN21 3UN by
Richard Clay Ltd, Bungay, Suffolk
Typeset by Nuprint Ltd, Harpenden, Herts

Contents

	Preface: Hidden Treasure	7
1	The Day of Opportunity	13
2	Time to Move	21
3	Facing the Unknown Alone	33
4	A Time to Weep	47
5	On the Shelf	63
6	Look Out! You're Being Followed	75
7	There's No Place Like Home	87
8	Good Company	103
9	Learning to Know God	111
10	Everything's Gone Wrong	121
11	God at Work for Good	131
12	God's Abundance	139
13	Put on Your Best Clothes	149
14	What Am I Worth?	157
15	Wedding Bells and Lasting Joy	167
16	Serving the Purpose of God	179

Preface

Hidden Treasure

It's wonderful how the Bible speaks so directly to us. It is always up to date and relevant. Often I have been surprised and thrilled when a verse in the middle of some obscure passage suddenly jumps off the page. I may not have fully understood the rest of the chapter, but that verse was just what I needed from the Lord.

Not long after my conversion, when I had only a limited knowledge of the Bible, I began attending a Christian college. The woman who was principal of the college led us through the Bible, book by book, in a two-year course. I was fascinated. The Old Testament came alive as I saw the thread running through the history of Israel that foretold the coming of the Messiah. The strange sacrifices in Leviticus portrayed the cross and became illustrations of the completeness of my salvation in Christ. I was grateful for those two years of study, for I gained an intellectual grasp of the Bible. My appetite was stimulated, and I began reading the Bible regularly from cover to cover.

At the time, though, what I learned was mostly 'head knowledge'. It was some years later that the

Holy Spirit began turning my mental understanding into a heart revelation. Only later in life, when the Holy Spirit allowed these truths to surface again, did I actually apply them.

Such has been the case with the Book of Ruth. I have read this delightful story many times without God saying anything particularly significant to me. But a few years ago, the story came alive. This time Naomi, not Ruth, stood out as the key character. Seeds were sown in my heart that have borne fruit in the lessons I will unfold in these pages.

God so often uses our circumstances to teach us his ways. As I've written about the principles we can draw from Naomi's life, I've used personal examples and insights I've gained in my years of walking with God in the roles of wife, mother, and now widow.

My husband, Arthur, and I shared thirty-nine years of ministry before his death in 1988. Arthur had a full-time writing and itinerant speaking ministry, and in later years he was part of an apostolic leadership team based at The Community Church in Southampton. In all, Arthur wrote eleven books on such subjects as revival, living a radical Christian life, and the underground church in China. His best known work is *God's Chosen Fast*, a guide to prayer and fasting that became a bestseller.

Through the years, I was involved in helping Arthur with his manuscripts, little dreaming that I would write books myself one day. My first book, *Queen Take Your Throne*, a women's book on the story of Queen Esther, arose out of some talks I had given to women. This book, also designed for women's study groups, follows a similar format.

The need for this book became apparent several years ago when Arthur and I gained increasing awareness of the pressures facing many Christians as they enter their middle and senior years. In a variety of churches, we discovered a disturbing trend among people forty and older. Among this age group, people who have such enormous potential for healthy life, we found a widespread feeling that life's best had already passed them by. Many saw little to look forward to in the years ahead. They faced the future with dread rather than expectation. If someone hadn't become a home group leader, an elder, or a deacon in his church by the time he had reached forty, then he felt that he had no worthwhile contribution to make, no value to the kingdom.

Arthur and I responded in part by planning a Bible Week seminar designed for those over forty. We chose the title, 'The Best Half of Life'. We determined to do all we could to dispel the myth propounded by current popular opinion that life holds no new horizons once you pass forty. I believe God was showing us, and others as well, the desperate need to awaken in this older generation new hope and confidence. We began to observe other churches gathering groups of mature believers together, encouraging them, and making use of them in ministry. During this time the lessons I was learning about Naomi became for me what I call a 'now word', a revelation with a specific message relevant for the church in our time.

Yet this book isn't only for the over-forty crowd. The story of the older woman, Naomi, is interwoven with the experience of her young daughter-in-law, Ruth. As the story of their adventure together unfolds, every age group can discover some valuable treasures.

I suggest you begin by reading the Book of Ruth just to enjoy the drama of this compelling story. It begins with Naomi as a wife in Israel who has everything a godly woman could desire. Even her name means 'delight'. When famine strikes, her husband decides to find relief by taking his family to the land of Moab. While there, Naomi's two sons marry Moabite women. But before these new couples have any children, Naomi's sons and her husband die.

It's obvious that during her years in Moab Naomi has maintained the same strong faith in Jehovah. Yet she feels she has nothing to offer her two daughters-in-law, who are obviously quite fond of her and whom she loves as well.

Naomi has made such an impression on Ruth that Ruth makes the most significant choice of her life. She pleads with Naomi to let her go with her to Israel. Ruth wants to live where Naomi lives; she wants Naomi's God to be her God. The enormous influence of this older woman is demonstrated in this startling decision. In following Naomi, Ruth chooses to abandon her family, her heritage, and a familiar culture for a foreign land with all the uncertainties awaiting two impoverished women without homes or husbands.

The two women eventually reach Israel, where Ruth goes out to glean in the fields and meets her future husband, Boaz. Naomi has a profound effect on Ruth, awakening her faith in God and turning her life in a direction that led to marriage with a prosperous, kind-hearted man. Scripture records that the grandchild of this blessed marriage— Naomi's great-grandson by marriage—was the father of none other than King David, an ancestor of the Lord Jesus Christ himself.

The widow Naomi, for whom life seemed to hold no future, discovered to her great joy that God was faithful to restore her life and provide great blessings to her in her old age. She discovered that God's greatest purpose for her was destined to be fulfilled in her later years.

This marvellous story is set in an ancient culture. Though the lifestyle of that era seems strange, I can identify with the principal characters and the situations they faced. These two women experienced feelings common to us all: the ache of grief; the sting of adversity; the comfort of each other's companionship; the joy of discovering the goodness and mercy of God. I hope that you, too, can identify with these biblical characters as you join me in search of hidden treasures. God's word is full of it.

At the end of each chapter I have included a short Bible study designed either for individual or group study. You might find it helpful to have a notebook to jot down key statements or passages and to describe what the Lord is teaching you. I find that taking notes helps me absorb the material and retain it longer. Some readers, of course, may prefer to ignore the studies and simply read straight through. However you proceed, pray for the Book of Ruth to come alive for you and for the Lord to give you a true revelation of the truths of his word.

1

The Day of Opportunity

The pile of letters the postman pushed through my letter-box looked unusually bulky. My curiosity aroused, I collected them, eager to discover their contents. I sorted through the magazines and junk mail and glowed with pleasure at the sight of familiar handwriting on one letter.

As I sat down at the table to eat breakfast before going through my letters, one large envelope cried out for immediate attention. 'Open now! Do not miss your great opportunity. You have been personally selected, Mrs Wallis.'

These words ought to have stirred me to immediately investigate this 'great opportunity'. But I had seen it before. I knew it was yet another elaborate effort to tempt me to spend my money. My suspicions proved correct. The makers of some thermal underwear, boasting that their brand was used by mountain climbers and was guaranteed to keep me warm in the most frigid temperatures, were urging me to buy now and prepare for the worst. What's more, if I acted within the next two weeks, I had the chance of winning £25,000. They even sent me a lucky number!

Summer was still with us; I was well supplied with winter undies and had no intention of climbing mountains. So without a qualm, I chucked the envelope into the nearest waste-paper basket so I could enjoy my breakfast in peace.

I receive piles of similar offers, each warning me not to miss out on a fantastic 'once-in-a-lifetime' opportunity. One day I calculated I could have won more than £110,000—if I had only responded.

Life is more than food, furniture, and fancy gadgets. Jesus tells us not to be anxious about these things because our heavenly Father knows our needs exactly and has promised to supply them. That's why I can throw away these offers knowing I have not thrown away an opportunity.

Opportunities to serve God

Consider for a moment the spiritual opportunities that have come your way. Can you look back to a day when you eagerly responded to a stirring sermon that challenged you to be ready to fulfil your destiny? Maybe you felt God calling you to do the work of an evangelist in your neighbourhood or community. Maybe you felt a desire to meet a special need in the church—teaching the children, befriending lonely singles, encouraging the downhearted, going on a short-term mission trip. We may want to respond, we may desire to do something significant for the kingdom; but without our knowing why, sometimes time goes by and nothing happens. This can occur again and again as we're presented with opportunities to serve the purpose of God. As we grow older, we're reminded of all those times when we didn't see God use us in a way that seemed significant.

Perhaps you're still wondering how God is going to make you his instrument, still wondering how you're going to fulfil your destiny. As time passes, the fear that you might have already thrown away the best opportunities the Lord has given you might quench your desire to press on with what you're doing now or to serve God in some new capacity.

We are tempted to give up on God because we fail to see our situation from his perspective. The postal adverts say, 'It's now or never.' If you don't respond in ten days, you're out of luck. That isn't the way God works; he doesn't give us any deadlines. He's using us all the time to fulfil his purpose. If opportunities pass by for whatever reason—due to our mistakes and shortcomings or from something beyond our control—God hasn't wasted the time. He uses every circumstance to shape us into ideal instruments for his handiwork.

The pile of letters that came that particular morning included a letter from a friend who was serving the Lord overseas. God had spoken to her during a stirring message at a Bible Week one summer and planted within her a longing to go overseas. Arthur and I prayed with her about her desire. But as time passed, no opportunities opened for her.

Wasted years?

Other areas of this woman's life weren't going according to plan, either. As the years went by, nothing seemed to be working out for her. Many of

her friends were getting married, but she was
approaching forty and was still single. Many of her
desires remained unfulfilled, and she was tempted
to give up. Finally the opportunity came to work in
the country she wanted. Though it was for only a
year, she seized it gratefully.

God used that waiting period to develop a
greater spiritual depth in her. He used that year
abroad to bless her and make her a blessing to
others, but also to shape her for the next opportunity. She found a fulfilling involvement in a pas-
toral team of her church, serving in all sorts of
practical ways. Africa might sound like a more
glamorous place to serve the Lord than a local
church, but doing God's will wherever he chooses
is the most satisfying course.

Having recently returned from a few years in a
remote area of Nepal, another fine young woman
was sharing her experiences with some older Christians. It had been a challenging but fruitful time,
and she'd left some of her heart behind. Should she
go back again? As she asked them to pray for her,
she frankly admitted the dilemma facing her.
Among other issues, she faced the fact that to do so
seemed like choosing to remain single for the rest of
her life. That is no easy choice, but God's will is
always good, pleasing and absolutely perfect (Rom
12:2). Because her heart is set to obey him, I am
confident that whatever her decision, she won't be
missing an opportunity.

There are times when responding to God's
opportunity appears to mean missing another good
one. The chance of promotion comes just after you
have been thrilled to be entrusted with the leader-

ship of an aspect of service that is close to your heart, but promotion involves relocation. The holiday of your dreams is offered to you, but you have already committed yourself to spending your vacation with a group giving practical help to needy Christians overseas. Such choices often have life-changing consequences, but we need never fear that choosing God's plan means something good is lost and gone for ever. 'No good thing does he withhold from those whose walk is blameless,' Psalm 84:11 reminds us.

The older we are, the easier it is to feel that life's opportunities are passing us by, especially if we are in a church with a large number of young people. 'Nothing has ever come of our eagerness in the past,' people tell themselves, 'so why not leave it to others much younger or more gifted than we are?' No age group is immune from the temptation to give up when it doesn't seem as if God is using them. In this 'instant' society we're programmed to expect everything to happen without delay—and without much effort. Computers provide instant answers that take the grind out of mathematics. We're accustomed to thinking that anything that saves time and eliminates work is progress.

The Lord, however, operates with a different agenda and timetable. God's opportunities are not put before us as instant packages for fulfilling our destiny in the kingdom. Serving his purpose is a lifetime process that begins the moment we respond to the challenge. 'Teach us to number our days aright,' Psalm 90:12 says, 'that we might gain a heart of wisdom.' It's a mark of wisdom to see every day as a day of significance and meaning and not

always be looking forward to some 'important day'
in the future. God says that now is the day of
salvation, and 'now' is always the day of opportunity.

God does not change his mind or cast us aside for
someone more suitable. He does not present us
with opportunities to be seized within two weeks
or two years or for ever lost. The apostle Paul tells us
that we can be completely confident that God's
desire is to complete the good work he has begun in
us—not just now, but right through to the end of
our days.

Whom can God use?

What kind of women does God choose? Someone
like Mother Teresa? A person with a famous name
or charismatic personality? An eloquent speaker? A
dedicated missionary? Of course such people have a
part to play in the kingdom, but the Bible teaches
that they are a minority. Most of the women whose
names we find recorded in the Bible were ordinary
mothers and daughters, housewives and working
women with whom we can all identify. That was
the case with Naomi, a woman who had no special
position, vocation, or talents. Nothing about her set
her apart from any ordinary woman of her time.

Many of us have the misconception that 'serving
the Lord' involves a prominent position or some
obvious label. We can look at someone in a high-
profile position in a church, and think that because
we don't have much visibility or responsibility,
we've missed our opportunity. But we're not all
called to be Bible study teachers or worship leaders.

We're called to be women of God. We so often think
we have to *do* something to be worthwhile, but God
just wants us to *be*. Doing is limited by our capacity
and opportunity; being a woman of God is a lifelong state.

Sometimes we can be looking for some great
opportunity instead of, like Naomi, seeing that God
is using us as ordinary people living for God day by
day. So you haven't missed out on anything, no
matter what your age, when you don't have a title
describing how you serve the Lord. Forget the
labels; there's always a golden opportunity awaiting every woman who desires to follow Jesus Christ
with her whole heart. If you have a heart that's
surrendered to Jesus, then whatever you're doing—
whether it's washing dirty dishes or speaking to an
audience of thousands—you're serving God.

Naomi and Ruth, the two main characters in the
Book of Ruth, provide just the encouragement we
need to be fully assured that God has a fulfilling
purpose for us, whatever our age. As we study this
book together may those who have lost the glory of
their youth begin to glow afresh with the enjoyment of their maturity. Then those who are still
young will be inspired to look to the future with
anticipation, free from any apprehension about
growing older. For all of us, the best days are still to
come. In God, there is plenty of time to seize our
opportunity.

Bible Study: The light that grows brighter

Proverbs 4:18 is a good verse to learn by heart. What
does it teach us about God's plan for our lives?

1. Does this verse support the belief that the days of our youth are the brightest and best and that opportunities diminish with every passing year?

2. Discuss or make a note of what you understand to be 'the full light of day'. Philippians 3 will help you.

3. Psalm 119:105, John 8:12 and 1 John 1:7 show us how to find help along 'the path of the righteous'. What other scriptures can you add?

4. What kind of people qualify for God's opportunities? See 1 Corinthians 1:26–29.

5. God has chosen you for a life full of many opportunities. Remind yourself of his wonderful plan as you read the following scriptures: Ephesians 1:4–5,11–12; 2:10. Find some other verses that confirm this.

2

Time to Move

In the days when the judges ruled, there was a famine
in the land, and a man from Bethlehem in Judah,
together with his wife and two sons, went to live for a
while in the country of Moab. The man's name was
Elimelech, his wife's name Naomi, and the names of
his two sons were Mahlon and Kilion. They were
Ephrathites from Bethlehem, Judah. And they went to
Moab and lived there (Ruth 1:1–2).

Names conjure up memories. 'Cora' for instance,
reminds me of my nursing days, when I cared for a
young woman in the WAAF with this name. Her
surname was Crow! I remember another patient
named Isobella who was always so grateful for
every little attention she received from the nurses
and insisted on giving us her precious chocolate
ration. 'Joe' reminds me of an uncle I never met,
who was killed during the war. As a child his photo
fascinated me, for he had one grey eye and one blue
eye.

Probably none of us in the Western world attach
as much importance to names as Hebrew parents
did in biblical times. Children's names were care-

fully selected to satisfy not only their parents' desires, but all the relatives' as well.

When a lovely girl was born in Bethlehem, she gave such joy to all who saw her that her parents named her Naomi. By this choice they were not only expressing their own pleasure but the family's expectation that this girl's future life would be like her name, which means 'pleasant'. This choice was a declaration of hope that the child was destined to be one on whom the favour of God would rest.

Ruth is a name popular with many Christian parents today, but I have not met many girls named Naomi. Ruth is associated with a young woman, whereas Naomi represents someone older. Is the fact that we have few children named Naomi an indication that we have been influenced by the modern tendency to associate youthfulness with success? When we look more closely at Naomi's life, we will discover her biggest success came in her later years. And though Naomi's young daughter-in-law is often the focus of study in the Book of Ruth, without Naomi, the book could never have been written.

As Naomi grew up, the hopes of her parents were fulfilled, and her life followed a favourable path. Married to a godly husband to whom she had borne two sons, Naomi apparently had everything a Hebrew woman valued. Her husband's name, Elim-elech, meant 'God is King'. Their home was a secure oasis in a period of unrest and lawlessness.

Hopes and fears for their nation

Elimelech and Naomi must often have talked together about their hopes and fears for Israel. When would the wonderful promises given to Abraham be fulfilled? Joshua, their great leader of old, had taken the Israelites into the land of promise where there was an abundance of food and plentiful water for the crops. No enemy nation could withstand the tribes of Israel because Jehovah was the One who gave them victory. But Naomi must have shuddered as she recalled all the things she'd heard about that took place after Joshua died.

She probably found it hard to believe that her ancestors had worshipped the idols of the nearby heathen nations and had joined in all their wicked practices. How could they burn little children as sacrifices? Then there were those horrible accounts of murder and rape. Joshua had challenged the nation before he died to choose between serving the Lord Jehovah and bowing to idols (Josh 24:14–15). The sad state of affairs was the inevitable result of the people failing to obey God and to love him with all their hearts.

In spite of all their vows to serve the Lord, the generations after Joshua forsook God and continued in idolatry. As a result the nation constantly suffered defeat at the hands of its enemies. From time to time, a ruler or judge arose who rallied the people. When they cried out to God to save them, in his great mercy he did so. But there was no lasting peace. Israel had no king, and every man did what was right in his own eyes (Judg 21:25). Yet there was still a remnant of godly men and women, like Elimelech and Naomi, whose hope rested in Jehovah's

promise to give them the land of Canaan and
deliver them from their enemies. They longed for a
godly king to govern them justly and free them from
constant strife.

Destined to be God's instruments

Little did Naomi know what an important part she
had to play in the realisation of Israel's longing for
peace and righteousness. The Book of Ruth is the
story of how two ordinary women became instruments in the fulfilment of God's promise to Abraham that through his seed all the nations of the
earth would be blessed (Gen 12:2–3).

Was there something special about these
women? Didn't some extraordinary event, miracle,
or revelation cause Naomi to have a sense that she
had been chosen for a divine and glorious purpose?
There's no evidence to support that idea. Naomi
was nothing more than we can be, by God's grace.
That's why this story is so encouraging. Naomi
appears to have been a normal, happily married
wife whose life centred on caring for her husband
and two sons. She had no special awareness of what
might be in store for her or how she might be used
to bring God's plan to pass; she just lived life as it
unfolded day by day.

None of us knows what lies around the corner.
It's good to throw ourselves wholeheartedly into
fulfilling our roles, whether we are married or
single. But we always need to keep alert, confident
that God is at work in our ordinary, even mundane,
circumstances, bringing about his glorious purpose. As believers, we are part of the fulfilment of

that promise to Abraham; we are the 'seed' through whom God is going to bless the nations. Together with Naomi, we have been chosen for a purpose.

So as we consider the lessons Naomi and Ruth have for us, let fresh hope be stirred in our hearts. The future is bright when we walk in the centre of God's will.

The daily routine

Imagine Naomi as she went about her daily duties, preparing the meals, caring for her sons, and helping in the fields. No cloud loomed on her horizon. No doubt she had plenty of friends, many of whom envied her good fortune.

One year, though, the crops failed. Drought or disease continued to plague the nation year upon year, food grew scarce, and famine settled in. Fear gripped women's hearts, and Naomi began to feel insecure for the first time in her life. Put yourself in Naomi's place, and imagine how you would feel if you and your family were going hungry. How would you have responded?

Elimelech faced the situation. Apparently they had plenty of money in hand, but no one had food to sell. Famine had not hit Moab, so Elimelech decided to move his family there until the crisis passed. If he was a potter, as some suggest, then he could rely on his skills to support his family. Naomi trusted her husband's judgement. They needed to go where they could provide their family with adequate food. Any apprehension about leaving relatives and friends was overshadowed by thoughts of famine's dreadful consequences. The

threat of starvation forced them to brush aside any
qualms about leaving the land of promise, the place
of God's covenant blessing, to live among a heathen
people. It was, after all, a temporary measure. They
would return to Bethlehem.

Naomi prepared to move. With mixed feelings,
she sorted out what to take and what to leave
behind. Every task served to underscore the
implications of this journey on which they were
embarking. So much concerning her daily life was
about to change. How would she feel in a strange
land away from her dear friends who had come to
say goodbye, lend a hand, and share a last frugal
meal together? What kind of neighbours would she
meet? How would they receive her? What customs
would these people observe? Her mind was probably buzzing with questions. Only the confidence
that it was 'just for a while' enabled her to keep up
an appearance of buoyancy. In spite of a tearful
farewell, her friends probably concluded this was
just another example of how Naomi always seemed
to have everything going for her. Now when all the
others were facing a bleak prospect, she was about
to escape. Once more they envied her going off to
face an exciting future. Years later, she described
her departure, saying, 'I went out full.'

Ready to move on

Naomi's departure reminds me of our last move.
We no longer needed as large a house, and Arthur
and I were looking for something smaller and more
economical. We knew the time had come to go on to
the next phase in our ministry. I had been delighted

with the home, but I knew our lives were moving on and I couldn't cling to it. A friend of mine asked, 'Don't you feel sad at leaving this lovely home?' She was ready to be full of sympathy because the house was the nicest we'd ever owned. But without hesitating, I replied, 'Not at all. God has taken this house right out of my heart, and I am eager to move to the place of his choice.'

There is no better place to be than right in the centre of God's will. For many years, Arthur and I lived in a beautiful county in southern England. We would visit homes and churches in the industrial areas of the north and enjoy the warmth and friendliness of the people. But as we drove along the busy motorways back to our quiet country home, we would often heave a sigh of relief that we were not called to live there. The south was home to us, and we could not imagine being anywhere else. Many exciting things had taken place in our home, and a young church had been born in the small town where we lived. Surely God would not want us to move! But yes, he would, we learned. We had unconsciously slipped into a rut, and he was going to bring us out of it by moving us, of all places, to the industrial north!

This move turned out to be a watershed in our lives; we looked back on that time as the beginning of a new and much more fruitful stage in our service for God. Knowing we were obeying him gave us a peace that had nothing to do with the circumstances. We found that his will is always perfect. We thoroughly enjoyed the years spent in what turned out to be a beautiful part of the country. Our old

situation no longer exerted any pull on our heart-
strings, and we never wanted to go back.

A testing time

Leaving Bethlehem for Moab was a major upheaval
for Naomi. It would not have been her natural
choice, but she knew God was with her as they set
up home in a foreign land inhabited by idol wor-
shippers. Naomi's faith was tested. She needed to
rely on spiritual resources, grace and strength, more
than ever before. Her roots of trust grew deeper as
she reached down into the steadfast love and
faithfulness of God. Now she began to understand
the reality of knowing him to be her rock and a very
present help in time of trouble (Ps 46:1). These were
invaluable lessons for the future.

Naomi soon realised that she would have to
make a clear choice between serving her Lord with
her whole heart or following the ways of her neighbours. It wasn't easy, but she never wavered in her
determination to be unashamed of her faith. Her
zeal for God could have isolated her from her neighbours and made her feel lonely at times, but it
proved to be crucial to God's purpose. It turned out
that what mattered most was the strong and lasting
relationship Naomi made with her two daughters-
in-law.

The Bible doesn't say directly what influence
Naomi had on people in Moab. But we are told that
she lived a life devoted to God, despite the intense
pressure to conform to the corrupted values of those
around her. Through her words, deeds, and attitudes, Naomi demonstrated her faith in a living

God. Be assured, your daily relationship with God affects people.

Naomi is a good example for us when we face a new job or new neighbourhood where people have no desire for God and have adopted lifestyles totally different from our own. Naomi became a light in that part of Moab because she had the courage to be true to her Lord.

Now, centuries later, we are participants of the blessing that resulted from Naomi's steadfast faith. Isn't that a stimulus for us to follow her example? If you find yourself surrounded by people who don't know the Lord, recognise that God has put you there for a purpose. Be a light shining the goodness, grace, and mercy of God into your situation. Do not yield to the temptation to become like those around you. First Peter tells us, 'As obedient children, do not conform to the evil desires you had when you lived in ignorance. But just as he who called you is holy, so be holy in all you do; for it is written: "Be holy, because I am holy" ' (1 Pet 1:14–16). Likewise, Romans 12:2 says, 'Do not conform any longer to the pattern of this world, but be transformed by the renewing of your mind.'

Being all things to all people to win them for Christ never means compromising our convictions. We cease to be a light for Jesus when we conform to the habits and values of the people around us.

And so we leave Naomi dealing with the stress of strange new circumstances, having moved under pressure to a new home in a foreign culture rife with ungodly influences. Yet what seemed to be a crisis robbing her of her highest hopes and dreams eventually proved to be the gateway to something much better.

Bible Study: God's will is to be enjoyed, not endured

Begin this study by practising two verses to commit them to memory: Romans 12:1–2. The constant repetition required to memorise a verse, especially if your brain is getting a bit rusty like mine, is a valuable aid to meditation. Let your mind dwell on scriptures that speak to you in a special way, hide them in your heart, and get all the goodness out of them. It's so easy in these days to allow ourselves to be caught up in the bustle and only have time to get a little taste of God's word, rather than the strong nourishment that is available. Meditation has been likened to the way a cow chews the cud. Wise creature!

Romans 12:1–2 gives us two keys for proving that God's will is best for us.

1. Offer yourself unreservedly to him as Lord (v 1; see also Rom 6:12–13). What do you think this means? Why does Paul refer to this as true worship? Is knowing God's will essential only when making important decisions?

2. Be transformed in your mind (v 2). Resistance to the will of God is centred in the mind. Renewal means changing from self-centredness to centring one's life on God. The fruit of a self-centred mind is apprehension about the future, fear of what God may demand, and a lack of peace and security. But a God-centred mind is ruled by the fear of the Lord. That goes hand in hand with the desire to please

him and the confidence of knowing his will (see Ps 25:12).

God's will is always in keeping with his character. That is why the fear of the Lord is so crucial. It goes hand in hand with wisdom, understanding and friendship with God (Ps 25:14, RSV). If someone I love and respect asks me to do something, I am eager to respond. It's a different story when that request comes from a person I distrust. Feeding my mind with scriptures that teach me how wonderful my God is and how perfect his character, will set me free to obey gladly and enjoy his will.

Make a list of verses about God's character. You will find many in the Psalms. Keep them in your notebook and use them to feed your faith in time of need. Psalm 145 is a good place to start.

3

Facing the Unknown Alone

Now Elimelech, Naomi's husband, died, and she was left with her two sons. They married Moabite women, one named Orpah and the other Ruth. After they had lived there about ten years, both Mahlon and Kilion also died, and Naomi was left without her two sons and her husband (Ruth 1:3–5).

One beautiful morning in August, I was looking forward to joining others in my church for a time of worship in the open air. As everyone knows, English weather is notoriously unpredictable; we never can be sure just when summer will arrive or how long it will last. So I was revelling in the prospect of enjoying the sunshine without having to take a raincoat just in case. After one of the wettest Julys in decades, our soggy spirits had been lifted when the sun drove the clouds away and embraced the earth in its warming gaze. We were in the midst of a week of evangelistic outreach, and instead of the usual Sunday morning service, the whole church had been encouraged to gather on the common, a large park and recreation area in the city. Many families would be there having picnics and relaxing, and we were praying that some would be attracted by our worship.

The phone rang just as I was about to leave. It was the son of a dear friend of mine, with news that early that morning his mother had died. Mollie had been in the last phase of a rare disease and had suffered for several months. I had treasured our friendship; that was evidence in the ache I felt inside when the reality began breaking upon me that in this life we would never again be together. Yet as much as I would miss her, I knew she was experiencing the joy of being with Christ, which, as Paul said, is 'far better'. My heart went out to her son and to her husband who would be feeling even deeper sorrow on this lovely morning. I prayed for Mollie's family and knew that they would be experiencing a comfort beyond human explanation. How wonderful it is at such times to be upheld by our Saviour's love.

Arthur and I lived in a quiet residential area of Southampton, within easy walking distance of the common. We often walked along the wooded paths and out into the open spaces of this lovely area. We greatly valued the beauty, fresh air, and exercise, which were so accessible. This particular weekend, Arthur was away, and I had plenty of time for meditation as I strolled through the trees and down the main avenue to where the people from the church were gathering. The deep blue sky and warm sunshine lightened my heart. Having death strike so near made me feel glad to be alive, yet my thoughts kept turning heavenward.

I had a wonderful time of worship that morning. I rejoiced to see the church family together, sur-

rounded by the beauty of God's creation, singing
his praises. Gathered here were little ones in push-
chairs with life before them, older people nearing
the end of their days sitting down, and those in the
full flush of life, with little thought of eternity,
standing or even dancing as they worshipped. I
couldn't stop thinking about Mollie. She had always
had a special place in my life, for she had first
introduced me to my Saviour. We met at school
when we were just eleven years old. I received the
Lord after Mollie invited me to Crusaders, a Sunday
afternoon Bible class for girls. She was a leader in
our school, and her whole-hearted devotion to the
Lord and bold witness to her classmates made quite
an impression on me. I thanked the Lord again for
her and all I owed to her influence in those for-
mative years.

That morning, a new richness was added to our
worship, a foretaste of that day when myriads from
every tribe, language, and nation shall worship the
Lamb that was slain. We shall all be together for
ever and ever. How desolate, indeed, are those who
sorrow without this glorious hope.

All of us must face bereavement. It is a needful
reminder that we are not an earthly people but
citizens of a heavenly kingdom. When we experience the frailty of life, we find it easier to set our
affection on things above rather than things below,
and our hold on material possessions is loosened.

Mollie's death caused me to reflect on the day
two years before, when for the first time I felt the
sudden loss of someone very dear to me. We were
in Portland, Oregon, where Arthur had been speaking at a church conference. Our hosts took great

pains to ensure that we had every opportunity to
take in the beauty of the Pacific northwest as well as
to enjoy good fellowship with church leaders. Ern
Baxter was also teaching, so we had a rich diet of
spiritual food, and by the end of the week we were
reluctantly preparing to move on to the next
engagement. Then, as we were sitting down for
breakfast the last morning, the phone rang. It was
our son, Jonathan, with heartbreaking news. Our
dear grand-daughter Katrina had died.

We were numb. It didn't seem possible that this
healthy fourteen-year-old was gone—someone so
lovely, so full of promise, with so much life before
her. Ern and Ruth Baxter were staying at the same
motel, and they very lovingly provided the immediate comfort we needed. Our hearts were heavy as
we shared our news with the leaders of the church.
Soon all who attended the meetings were aware of
what had happened. We were sustained by the loving concern and practical care of God's people. They
made our travel arrangements, and within a few
hours we were on a flight back to London to be with
our family. It still blesses me to remember how
people at the church—most of them total
strangers—came to hug us, pray with us, and weep
with us as we bade them farewell. What healing
balm lies in the love of God's precious people. As
with Mollie's death, Katrina's passing made heaven
seem so much nearer.

Arthur and I attended the funeral and thanksgiving service for Mollie, my friend who had served
her Saviour so faithfully. It was held at the church
where her husband, now retired, had been the pastor for many years. Hundreds came to express their

love and comfort to her husband and to praise God for the influence of Mollie's life. We joined the relatives later at the home and met many old acquaintances with whom we had lost touch as our paths had diverged. What a joy to renew friendships and have a taste of the 'family' reunion already taking place for those who have departed this life.

I was especially pleased to remember the last time I had seen Mollie alive. Three of us who had been friends at school had lunch at her house. We reminisced about old school days, and it was an occasion of much fun and laughter. We had not always agreed about spiritual issues in earlier years, and this had tested our friendship, but our love for one another had held firm. Death often alters our perspective on life. It causes us to see more clearly what is temporal and what is eternal; what is insignificant, and what is truly valuable. Love is more important than correct doctrine. The things that unite us as Christians far outnumber the things that divide. How assuring it is to have fond memories and no regrets when friends depart.

Tasting life's bitter side

The first thing we learn about Naomi's life in Moab is that Elimelech died, leaving the woman with her two sons to walk the path of sorrow alone, away from her family and friends. Who can understand the pain of losing a spouse? Only a widow knows what it's like to be widowed. Everything always had seemed to go right for Naomi; now for the first time she was tasting the bitter side of life. Perhaps she wished they had never left her homeland. If only she had known! But God uses life's bitter blows to give us confidence that even in the darkest hour of despair he will never abandon his children. Naomi might never have fully understood this had she remained in Israel and not ventured into the unknown.

Our all-loving, all-wise heavenly Father does not reveal every detail of the path before us. To do so would totally throw us off balance. We would either be jumping over the moon with excitement or sinking into the depths of despair, full of fear or worn out from the strain of preparing for what's to come. He knows we do best by learning to live one day at a time. As Matthew 6:34 advises, 'Do not worry about tomorrow, for tomorrow will worry about itself.' That, however, is not as easy as it sounds! How often have we lost sleep and gained extra wrinkles as we dreaded a situation that never came?

Every trial and hardship overcome victoriously by God's grace serves to strengthen us for the next. We become strong in faith, able to strengthen the weak and encourage those who feel like giving up. Those who are mature know that life will be a path of sadness as well as joy. But we can also know the truth Paul expressed in Romans 8:37–39: 'In all these things we are more than conquerors through him who loved us. For I am convinced that neither death nor life...nor anything else in all creation, will be able to separate us from the love of God that is in Christ Jesus our Lord.' I have been through several experiences I would have dreaded if I had known they were coming—the loss of two babies, surgery for cancer, the death of a grand-daughter, a dear friend, and a husband. In all these—in spite of all these—the reality of God's love and nearness was overwhelming. I can confidently say I've learned, as did the apostle Paul, that neither death nor disease nor anything else can separate me from the love of God.

Our heavenly Father knows when we are able to cope with trials, and he plans them as part of the process of shaping our characters and equipping us for his service. He saw the heart of Naomi, a woman who truly loved him, and recognised her as someone who could be entrusted with a measure of sorrow others might not have been able to bear. Though God had taken away her husband, Naomi still had two sons, giving her some masculine shoulders to lean on as she took over many of Elimelech's duties. Even so, it wasn't easy adjusting to the burden of all the new responsibilities and decisions.

A faith of our own

In our early married life Arthur was often away from home. It was not usually for more than a week at a time, but occasionally he was gone much longer and once even for nearly two years while he ministered in New Zealand. I joined him for a few months in the middle of that period, leaving our son behind with Arthur's mother. I learned a great deal during those months of separation. They were not something I would have chosen, but at the time I knew it was right. I had to trust God for myself and not lean on my husband's faith.

It's all too easy for wives to be so busy coping with the practical care of their homes and families that they opt out of any spiritual responsibility. After all, doesn't Scripture tell us (in Eph 5 and 1 Tim 3) that a man is to be a priest in his own household? True as that is, it behoves wives to cultivate their own relationship with God, to trust him ourselves and grow strong in faith. Being left alone taught me to go to God for help in those calamities that always seem to strike when I'm alone. As soon as my husband leaves, why must the washing machine flood, the drain clog, my child's bicycle be stolen, and the cat disappear? Minor incidents loom large at such times, but they teach us how much God really cares about us. If he counts the hairs of our heads and watches over every sparrow, then he also takes great delight in helping us cope, knowing our faith will be all the stronger.

I have vivid memories of a time when Arthur was travelling to South America. We lived then in an isolated bungalow on a Yorkshire farm. Flocks of sheep grazed on the surrounding fields, and early in the morning we could see rabbits coming out to play. No house was less than half a mile away, and the view across the distant moors was breathtaking. While the isolation made the home an idyllic place for writing or relaxing after a busy period of ministry, I worried about what would happen if I ever got into difficulties when I was there alone.

It was spring when Arthur left for Argentina. We'd had a mild winter and were enjoying unseasonably warm days, so I felt no qualms about staying behind. And it so happened that a friend had just arrived to spend a few days with me.

The day after Arthur left, though, a freak blizzard swept through the region, leaving a deep blanket of snow. The drifts blocked the lane to my house, and the storm had brought down the telephone lines. We were completely cut off from the outside world!

Stranded as we were, God showed his kindness and protection in so many ways that my friend and I could not but praise him. Many nearby homes lost their electricity for several days, but our power was spared. A kind local farmer made his way on foot through the snow to see if we were all right, and the next day ploughed his way to us by tractor. Within a few days it was possible to drive out again. Arthur had tried unsuccessfully to reach me by phone from Argentina, and when he heard at last that a blizzard had struck, he could hardly believe it. I took some photographs of the deep drifts just to prove I was not exaggerating!

We can only imagine all that Naomi had to handle alone, but one development must have made her miss Elimelech more than ever: her sons both fell in love with Moabite women. It was only natural that Mahlon and Kilion wanted to marry, and Naomi was undoubtedly eager for each of them to find a suitable partner. Should she urge them to go back to Bethlehem and find wives from their own nation? Or should she overlook the fact that Ruth and Orpah weren't Israelites and accept them into the family? What would Elimelech have done? Later events indicate that God gave her peace in this decision, and she grew to love her Moabite daughters-in-law.

Elimelech and Naomi must have looked forward to the time when their boys would marry and have families of their own. As a widow, Naomi must have waited in hope for her dream of being a grand-mother to come true. Grandchildren would help to fill the void she felt in her life, especially now that her sons had wives to care for them. But her dreams disappeared when both Mahlon and Kilion died. After living as a widow for ten years, Naomi suddenly had no children and no opportunity for grandchildren; nothing was left of the family except three widows. Naomi must have felt desolate. God, it seemed, had afflicted her with more than she could bear.

Orpah and Ruth needed strength and help from their mother-in-law. Naomi knew the ache they felt, and her heart went out to them. But how could these young women understand her great sorrow at losing first a husband and then two sons? The three women were a source of sustenance to each other. But as the oldest, and someone acquainted with grief, Naomi would give these women more than she received in this difficult hour. In life, experience is far more valuable than knowledge or theories; many lessons can only be learned by living. The older we are, the more we must expect to bear others' burdens.

Naomi was deeply concerned for her beloved daughters-in-law. To her it seemed she had nothing to offer them. She saw no future for herself in Moab and decided the time had come to return home. Her advice was that they stay behind.

Orpah wanted to go back with Naomi, but eventually Naomi persuaded her against it, and she departed weeping as she returned to her family. Naomi pleaded with Ruth to do the same, but Ruth was adamant: she would remain with Naomi. The loving devotion Ruth's determination showed must have been comforting to Naomi. And so the two of them set out together on the journey back to Bethlehem. The fact that two women travelled alone across the desert and arrived safely is evidence that God was watching over and protecting them.

Adversity: valuable preparation

God had allowed Naomi to experience intense sorrow, and he had proved himself to be a very present help in trouble. He did not forsake her; indeed, he was beside her, preparing her for her most fulfilling years. Naomi could not see anything ahead but adversity; the sorrow of the present clouded her judgement. But soon her eyes would be opened as God's amazing purpose for her life unfolded. God had given her the young woman who was the key to his plan coming to pass. He had brought Naomi and Ruth together because they needed each other. The mother in Naomi needed the encouragement and enthusiasm of the younger woman, and Ruth needed the stability and security an older woman can bring.

Bible Study: In God's hands

> God holds the key of all unknown,
> And I am glad.
> If any other hands should hold the key,
> Or if he trusted it to me,
> I might be sad.
>
> What if tomorrow's cares were here
> Without its rest?

I'd rather he unlocked the day
And as the hours swing open say,
'My will is best.'

I cannot read his future plans,
But this I know—
I have the smiling of his face
And all the refuge of his grace
While here below.

(J. Parker)

Having something to look forward to often enables
us to persevere through our present situation. But
most life-changing events come unexpectedly. The
words from this hymn remind us that our future is
in God's hands; there is no better assurance to set
our minds at rest. Unexpected situations cast us on
God's grace and test the reality of our faith. How
good it is to know that they are not taking God by
surprise, but have been carefully planned and
timed to enable us to get to know him more.

Psalm 139 is one of the best places in Scripture to
take hold of this truth. I have found it a source of
great comfort and strength when going through
some unexpected trial. If I were to choose a title for
Psalm 139, it would be 'The God who knows.' Read
it through slowly and carefully.
1. Note any particular verse that stands out for you.
2. Make a list of everything this psalm says that
God knows.
3. If you are in a group, share what you have found
and add to your list things you might have missed.
4. Discuss the implications of what you've found.
5. Verses 7 to 12 remind us that there is no place
where God cannot reach us. Write out verse 10, but

instead of the word 'there', describe the situation you find most hard and claim it as a promise. For example, write, 'Even in that office with my difficult boss your hand will guide me, your right hand will hold me fast.' Remember there is no place too remote, nor anything too difficult for God.

6. Say how God has helped you face difficult or unexpected situations.

4

A Time to Weep

Then Naomi said to her two daughters-in-law, 'Go back, each of you, to your mother's home. May the Lord show kindness to you, as you have shown to your dead and to me. May the Lord grant that each of you will find rest in the home of another husband.' Then she kissed them and they wept aloud (Ruth 1:8–9).

I struggled for two years to begin writing this book. Ideas were flooding my mind, and my file of material was growing thick. But whenever I sat down to write, I would hit a brick wall. Arthur did his best to encourage me, knowing how much I had studied and prayed for a fresh anointing for the task. Then one day I found a large object sitting on the table I used as a desk. Arthur had stuck a note on it that read, 'Now will you get on with it!'

The object was a word processor he had secretly purchased from a friend. This model was similar to one Arthur used, so he was able to teach me the basics. I had assumed that such a complicated machine was beyond me; I didn't count myself as part of the computer age. But God stirred me to rise to the challenge; I decided it's never too late to learn a new skill.

Progress was slow at first. But with Arthur close at hand and a reasonably clear instruction book, I began to master a new vocabulary. When I actually succeeded in producing my first article and printing it out, I was just bursting with pride! I completed three chapters of my book in the next three months, which seemed to me a tremendous achievement after my earlier difficulty. But then we were plunged into moving house, which squeezed out any opportunity for writing.

That interruption was extended for nearly a year by a circumstance that pushed my writing aside completely and brought personal matters to the forefront. My husband died unexpectedly from an apparent heart attack. 'Only a widow knows what it's like to be widowed.' I had written those words only a few weeks before Arthur died! In retrospect, I can understand why it was so hard for me to make much progress on this book. As Solomon said, there is a time for everything. In his infinite wisdom, God was waiting until I could identify with Naomi in her widowhood. Before Arthur died, I could only imagine Naomi's thoughts and emotions as she endured the death of her spouse and two sons and struggled to deal with all the ramifications. But passing over some of the same rugged terrain that Naomi travelled has given me much more insight into her life and circumstances.

Looking back, a statement I had written in Chapter 3, just before Arthur's death, seemed almost prophetic: 'Our all-loving, all-wise heavenly Father does not reveal every detail of the path before us. To do so would totally throw us off balance.' I would have been thrown off balance—indeed, devastated—by the prospect of losing the one I loved so dearly.

Arthur and I had looked forward to the years ahead in our new home, expecting this to be the most fulfilling and fruitful phase of our ministry together. Surprisingly, by the grace of God, I didn't question what God was doing. I trusted that God would fulfil his purpose, but I had to wait for him to reveal my future path.

God preparing the way

As I reflect on the months before Arthur's death, I can see God's kindness to me as he prepared our household for the transition that was soon to come. We had long felt the need for a smaller home and one nearer to our son and his family, and after months of searching, God led us to an attractive house just five minutes from our son's home. God knew how important it would be for me to have family close at hand.

For months Arthur and I had been going through our possessions, getting rid of unnecessary clutter and preparing ourselves for the move to a smaller home. An avid reader, Arthur owned hundreds of books and was always loath to reduce the size of his library. I knew what a sacrifice he was making when I saw him assigning a large number of books to be given away. They were his friends, but alas, he would have no room for them all. Once we were moved into our new home, one of the first projects accomplished was to arrange neatly Arthur's library; each book was classified by subject and put in its proper place.

Arthur had spent hours sorting through his old study, clearing his desk and files of unwanted papers, correspondence, and the like. A meticulous man, he habitually kept neat files of everything related to his work and to our household and financial affairs. Though I gave it little thought at the time, how grateful I would be later for his careful attention to detail.

Before moving into our new home, Arthur and I had made plans for redecorating. We bought several pieces of new furniture, as well as an oven. We chose all the costly items together, making several major decisions that I would have found difficult to make on my own. Almost every major item we needed was already purchased or picked out and ready for delivery. Having decided as well to build a brick garage with an attached archway leading into the back garden Arthur had asked a friend to draw up the building plans.

So everything was coming together: we had found a lovely home with a perfect location, our garage was planned, our furnishings purchased and ready for delivery. The prospect of being in this home and serving the Lord together filled me with great pleasure.

We had a full autumn ahead, starting off with a conference in Sheffield. Twelve days after we moved, I drove Arthur to the railway station to catch an early train; I was to join him in Sheffield two days later.

After dropping Arthur off, I went to a friend's house for our weekly time of prayer together. It was a warm, sunny day, and when I returned home, I enjoyed my work, unpacking more boxes and finding places to put things. I even found a few moments to relax in our lovely new garden. By the time evening came, I was ready for a good sleep and retired early.

At about 10:30 pm, the doorbell rang. I wondered who it could be at that late hour. I looked out of the window to see my son and his wife and two other men standing there. Filled with apprehension, I hurried downstairs to let them in. As gently as he could, my son broke the news that my beloved husband had died in Sheffield a few hours earlier.

It seemed so unreal; I couldn't take it in. I was numb with shock. But when I learned all the circumstances surrounding Arthur's death, I could not doubt that our heavenly Father had planned every detail of his final hours on earth.

Arthur's last day was a particularly happy one. In Sheffield he joined a group of his oldest friends, brothers in ministry, for a period of seeking God in prayer. The afternoon was spent praying for revival and sharing from the Scriptures on the centrality of Christ, two of his favourite themes. In the evening, he enjoyed happy fellowship around the dinner table. Afterwards he had great fun playing croquet, one of his favourite sports, and he won the game. 'Well done, Arthur,' a friend called to him. Then, as he walked over to help his partner, he went straight into the presence of Jesus. He collapsed at the side of the croquet lawn at the foot of a large wooden cross. Who else but his loving heavenly Father could have planned such a fitting end to Arthur's life?

That assurance was a tremendous source of strength to me in the difficult months that followed. It was God's time to call Arthur to be with Christ; therefore it was God's time for me to be alone. I was not just the unfortunate victim of my circumstances.

As I adjusted to all the new experiences life brought me, Psalm 139 became a living word:

> You have laid your hand upon me.... Where can I flee from your presence? If I go up to the heavens, you are there; if I make my bed in the depths, you are there.... If I say, 'Surely the darkness will hide me and the light become night around me,' even the darkness will not be dark to you; the night will shine like the day (Ps 139:5–12).

I am privileged to have brothers and sisters in the church who, along with my family, rallied around me at the time of crisis and continued to provide invaluable support. Yet I found that grief has to run its course. Even with the love and comfort of friends, feelings of loneliness set in. One friend in whom I confided this told me, 'Eileen, you've just got to walk through it.' And so I did, at times with faltering steps, but always upheld by an unseen hand.

Grief sometimes surfaces in unexpected ways. To my surprise, I could enjoy looking at family photographs or rummaging through Arthur's books. The memories were a delight to me. I would go along fine for a while, but then certain situations would trigger a wave of emotion. Driving the car was especially difficult. It was a responsibility of Arthur's I had to assume right away, and there was little way to avoid it. Driving along, the thought would hit me, 'I'll never be a passenger with Arthur driving any more.' It made me feel really low. Then I would think about how I was driving home to an empty house, and, invariably, I'd be weeping by the time I pulled into the driveway.

The fact of being alone is difficult to come to terms with. Very seldom would I go through a day without seeing somebody—a neighbour, a friend in the church, someone stopping by. Some days, of course, I'd see a lot of people. But then at the day's end, it was always the same—alone again. Sometimes I just longed to talk to Arthur. There were times when I went away for an exciting weekend of visiting friends, speaking at a church, or being involved in a women's weekend. I had some enjoyable, even thrilling, experiences. Then I would return home and the action suddenly stopped. The house was empty. There was no one to talk to. I was by myself again. Even after a weekend in which I had experienced the blessing of God, it was hard to feel a sense of God's purpose being fulfilled in my life.

It was hard facing situations in which the two of us had always been together. For instance, the first time I attended a weekend conference and stayed in a room alone was painful for me. I also found it difficult to walk on the common, where Arthur and I had taken walks together almost every morning. Those were especially meaningful times. As we talked, we often prayed in a conversational way about the people we knew and things that were happening in our church. After Arthur's death, I walked the paths alone and met a lot of retired couples walking arm-in-arm, as we had. I couldn't

bring myself to go to one particular area of the
common for many months. Because we had gone
there so often, I associated it with Arthur. Just driving past triggered my tears.

There were many deep valleys to tread, but God's
word was something secure I could hold on to in my
hour of grief. 'For I, the Lord your God, hold your
right hand,' Isaiah 41:13 says. 'It is I who say to you,
"Fear not, I will help you" ' (RSV). I clung to these
words and would often actually hold out my hand
to God, thanking him for having me in his grasp.

Arthur had died in September. Though I missed
him dearly and was very emotional, life was full
that autumn; I made a trip to the United States and
visited some friends. When I returned home and
the family celebrated its first Christmas without
Arthur, we were all feeling low. But for me, the first
few months of the new year were the deepest valleys. I had deep feelings of loneliness and felt totally
empty. It was mid-winter. The calendar was almost
blank. The days were short and dark. I didn't know
what I was going to do with myself.

In January, I went to a church leadership conference, the first I had ever attended without
Arthur. I was at my lowest ebb, desperately missing
Arthur and unsure of what life had for me. At that
time, during my daily Bible reading, God made one
verse stand out—Luke 6:21: 'Blessed are you that
weep now, for you shall laugh' (RSV). I counted that
as a precious promise God gave me to hold on to. I
knew it meant much more than just having some
fun. I'd enjoyed gatherings with my friends and
family and had had some good laughs. This was to
be something deeper. When Arthur died, the spar-

kle—'the delight of my eyes,' as Scripture says—
had gone out of my life. Even though I still had
times of fun and laughter, something was missing.
Arthur was gone. I couldn't imagine life ever being
the same again. I couldn't imagine that sparkle
returning. When God gave the promise of Luke 6:21
to me, he was saying, 'You're weak now, but the
sparkle will come back.' I couldn't understand how
God would do it, but I knew that only he could
bring this promise to pass. It was a challenge to me.
God was asking me to believe that I could find
greater joy in my relationship with him than I had
ever known before. So I held on to that and kept
asking God to fulfil his promise.

As my friend had said, I had to walk through my
grief. But as we walk into the 'valley of the shadow
of death', we discover that God is with us. He
doesn't shield us from sorrow or anaesthetise us
from the pain; rather, we find him in the midst of it.
Then, as the months and years go by, recovery takes
place and we feel the hurt easing. We don't miss our
loved ones any less, but over time the wound
begins to heal.

Life begins to emerge

As the winter months wore on, I went through ups
and downs as I gradually adjusted to life on my
own. When spring came, it seemed that all of life
began emerging again. My spirits picked up as I
began to write again and join in more activities.

The most important thing I learned from losing
my husband is how much we need to hold on to the
only relationship that can never be lost. God wants

us to love him with a whole heart. He loves us so much that he allows us to go through times of grief and testing in order to deepen that relationship. He is a jealous God who 'tolerates no rivals' (Deut 6:15, GNB).

As I sought the Lord with my whole heart, suddenly one morning I knew something had happened. There was a deep joy within that could not be explained. I was doing routine kitchen chores, and my heart was so full of praise I burst into song. I had been thinking about our fortieth wedding anniversary, which was coming in two days. Only God could have filled me with such eager anticipation. He had shown me that the best way to deal with the event would be to invite my friends to join me for a time of thanksgiving for the many happy years of married life with Arthur.

Our anniversary arrived on a beautiful sunny day, just like our wedding day, forty years before. But instead of plummeting into sorrow and loneliness, I had one of the happiest days I'd known since Arthur died. My family and friends made sure there was little for me to do but enjoy myself, and the cream on the strawberries came directly from my heavenly Father through his word. I've made a practice of reading through the Bible consecutively, and the passage I was due to read that day included these words in John 16: 'You will grieve, but your grief will turn to joy' (v 20) and 'Ask and you will receive, and your joy will be complete' (v 24). Moreover, a cross-reference led me to Job 29:13, which says, 'I made the widow's heart sing.' What more could I have asked?

Shortly after Arthur's death, I was not only emotionally numbed, but I felt spiritually paralysed. My mind wouldn't focus or concentrate on the Bible. It was humbling to be unable to draw water out of the wells of salvation. I needed to be spoon-fed! God's people were a vital source of strength; their words of comfort were life-giving. Sometimes just one Scripture verse from a friend, read over and over again, would minister to me.

I also enjoyed joining others in worship; to me it was a foretaste of heaven. That's where my beloved was, and one day we would all be together worshipping the Lamb upon the throne. I could imagine Arthur and Katrina in heaven, enjoying their reunion and fellowship with the Lord.

For those of us who have assurance of eternal life, thoughts of heaven are not mere fantasy. Indeed, they keep us from being earthbound in our thinking. I found that the perspective of eternity we have as Christians gave me a great opportunity to share my faith with my new neighbours. Several kind people came up to me and expressed their sympathies. 'It's quite a shock,' one neighbour commented. 'It's terrible that it happened so soon after you moved in.'

'Yes, it is,' I replied. 'But how wonderfully God has provided for me in that my son is only a few minutes away.' I continued, 'It's also a great comfort to have the confident hope that Arthur and I will be together again. He's not gone for ever. I'm going to see him again in heaven, and that assurance keeps me going.'

People might have a vague belief in life after death, but when you assert the truth with confidence, the reality of eternal life hits them and makes them wonder whether they could face death with the same confidence. One neighbour told me, 'I wish I had the faith you have.'

The fear of death looms large in the minds of many, and as Christians we can only give others cause to hope if we are set free from fear ourselves. Ecclesiastes 7:1 declares that the day of death is better than the day of birth! Do we really believe that?

Naomi's desperate hour

With her husband and two sons dead, Naomi was left without any of God's people to minister to her. She desperately needed to return to her homeland. News that the famine in Israel had passed confirmed to her that the time was right for this hazardous undertaking. Robbers were always ready to prey on lonely travellers, and to attempt the journey on her own must have seemed crazy. We can assume that Naomi clung to Jehovah in her hour of need, assured that he would make a way.

Ruth was also going through the most traumatic experience of her young life. Bereft of husband and childless as well, she had no real hope. A widow's life was difficult, often one of destitution. Ruth's own family, no doubt, would take her back. That was the most reasonable option. But something had happened deep within her, and she could never return to a heathen lifestyle. Her mother-in-law was broken-hearted and weary, yet had found something the Moabite gods could not offer, and Ruth was determined to follow Naomi's example. In setting her heart to seek the Lord, Ruth placed her feet on a path that would lead to the only certain answer to life's greatest trials.

Sooner or later, we all face something that seems to end our dreams and present a future without hope. Maybe you're facing the prospect of never getting married. Perhaps a business failure wipes out a life's savings or a serious illness strikes, putting the family's future in jeopardy. I've known women who have set their hearts on having children only to learn they're unable to bear any. Naomi and Ruth were facing such a seemingly hopeless situation. On their own, each might have foundered. But together, though neither realised it, they were heading towards the most fulfilling time of their lives. Have your dreams been shattered? Take heart even as you read this. Don't let your soul's enemy rob you of hope. The God who brought Naomi and Ruth safely to Bethlehem, to a place of blessing and joy, can do the same for you.

Be encouraged by the words of this old hymn:

> God moves in a mysterious way,
> His wonders to perform.
> He plants his footsteps on the sea
> And rides upon the storm.
> You fearful saints fresh courage take,
> The clouds you so much dread
> Are big with mercy and shall break
> In blessings on your head.
>
> (W. Cowper)

Bible Study: Looking forward to our destiny

1. Read Ecclesiastes 7:1–4 in the NIV, The Living Bible, and in any other version you have. Our destiny is clearly stated, and the wise will think about it while there is yet time. Before going any further, ask yourself if you have any good reason to look forward to your destiny. Now do some investigation on your own by looking up related scriptures. For starters, read Philippians 1:20–23, John 11:25–26, John 14:1–3, and Revelation 21:1–5.

2. Consider some reasons why it is important to think about this subject now.

(a) Man is born with a fear of death. Once during a radio programme on the topic of death and dying, I heard someone comment, 'The fear of death is so natural that all life is one long effort not to think about it.' Even Christians tend to avoid the subject! We have no need to fear, though, for Jesus has triumphed over sin and death by his own death on the cross and has destroyed the root of all fear. Read Hebrews 2:14–15. Now you can claim these promises for yourself. Read also John 8:31–32,36, Psalm 34:4, and 2 Timothy 1:7.

(b) The spirit is willing but the flesh is weak. We all need to be stirred and challenged to live a life pleasing to God. Discuss the implications of 2 Corinthians 5:9–10 and 2 Peter 3:13–14.

(c) Heaven is where we belong! The gift of eternal life assures us of a future far more wonderful than anything this life offers. Instead of fear, let's be filled with hope and anticipation. Read John 17:14,16,24, Philippians 3:20, and Hebrews 11:1–2,13–16.

End your study on a note of praise as you consider the hope proclaimed by these scriptures that death is the gateway to resurrection life.

5

On the Shelf

But Naomi said, 'Return home, my daughters. Why would you come with me? Am I going to have any more sons, who could become your husbands? Return home, my daughters; I am too old to have another husband. Even if I thought there was still hope for me—even if I had a husband tonight and then gave birth to sons—would you wait until they grew up? Would you remain unmarried for them? No, my daughters. It is more bitter for me than for you, because the Lord's hand has gone out against me!' At this they wept again. Then Orpah kissed her mother-in-law goodbye, but Ruth clung to her (Ruth 1:11–14).

'If in doubt, chuck it out.' My husband and I repeated that phrase the first time we ever moved. We had lived in that house twenty-five years and had accumulated a number of possessions that 'might be useful some day'. Now the moment of truth had come. It was time to clear out those dusty, seldom-used items once and for all. We made up our minds to be ruthless.

Both Arthur and I had to learn to curb the temptation to keep acquiring 'more stuff'. Arthur used to say he wanted to travel light, as far as this world's goods were concerned. After all, we leave everything behind when we depart, so why burden your descendants with clutter?

In spite of our good intentions, though, we still held on to some things long after they had any apparent usefulness. Tucked away and forgotten in the back of the cupboard or on a high shelf were a variety of ornaments, gadgets and various knick-knacks.

Arthur's area of weakness was his books, and mine was a collection of pebbles and shells. Whenever he found a secondhand bookshop he had not explored before I'd resign myself to the inevitable. Yet more books to add to his bulging shelves! I was equally guilty, though. As soon as the chance came to walk along the seashore on holiday, my pockets would be heavy before long with stones and shells of all shapes, sizes and colours.

Eventually both of us learned to overcome the temptation. Arthur's bookshelves contained only those he really did need, and my kitchen window-sill has a limited collection of my treasures that remind me of places we visited together.

In my present home, I have no spare shelves or cupboards available, so I have to be quite selective about what I keep around. Nevertheless there's a tempting space above my kitchen cupboards, and I have to confess that there are some things up there which just might be useful one day!

A few weeks ago I happened on a fondue set that Arthur had bought on a trip to Switzerland in the 1960s. I had hardly ever used it because whenever I suggested fondue, Arthur would say, 'No, let's have a proper meal.' He never thought a supper of bread and cheese would satisfy hungry guests. So the fondue pot remained in a kitchen cupboard year after year, looking quite decorative but never used. I had planned to get rid of it before our last move, but once again I stuck it on a shelf somewhere and forgot it.

Not long ago, though, I took the fondue set down and said to myself, 'Fondue is a delicious treat. I really ought to make use of this.' So I invited several single women for a get-together, with cheese fondue as the focal point of our meal. It was great fun. Suddenly, after sitting on the shelf for years, the fondue set came into its own and found a useful place in the household.

It's hard to admit it, but sometimes we feel like someone's forgotten possession, stuck away on a back shelf like my old fondue set. We become vulnerable, feeling left out and useless. Such feelings aren't uncommon; they surface for a variety of reasons. Perhaps several of your friends have been promoted to more exciting jobs, and you're still stuck in the same old routine. Or, after a lifetime of looking after your mate, you've become a widow and no longer feel needed or valuable.

Women in particular like to feel that somebody needs them; we want to be essential to someone's well-being. So when we hit our forties or fifties and children begin leaving the nest, it can be a struggle. Life can seem so empty when you no longer have people who depend on you or the responsibilities that once occupied much of your time: planning special meals, attending school activities, taking the kids to football or piano lessons.

Retirement can also make people think they're

being set aside. One might feel like an old memento stuck on a shelf, an object that reminds people of a past that is interesting, but irrelevant. Older people can suddenly have lots of free time with no one making use of it. If their potential is not tapped, they can feel lost, questioning whether life has purpose for them any longer. They fear they're in danger of being thrown into the rubbish dump like some ageing gadget that has outlived its usefulness.

Naomi was plagued by such feelings. She was convinced that life had passed her by and that she had nothing more to offer. 'Don't come with me,' she urged Orpah and Ruth. 'I'm not going to have any more children. I'm too old; no one will marry me now.' These words could have been uttered by some lovely women I know who long to be wives and mothers but see their chances of marriage rapidly diminishing. It isn't easy to watch your hopes fade as the years slip by. Every birthday is like a bell tolling the message, 'You're too old; you're on the shelf; no one wants you.'

Though spoken thousands of years ago, Naomi's words indicate she had slipped into believing some myths that are still a major source of frustration and discouragement for Christian women today. The first is that marriage is essential in order to serve God effectively. The second myth is that age disqualifies us. This is the notion that once we reach forty, we're on a downhill slope towards uselessness.

The later years of Naomi's life proved how false these assumptions were for her. They are equally false for us. It's hard to be optimistic when the gloomy facts of life seem to stare us in the face; hard to be buoyant when we see no changes in sight. But that's the time to take our eyes off our circumstances and fix them on a loving Father who delights to give good things to those who ask. Naomi, overwhelmed with grief, could see nothing but the painful circumstances in her life. She felt terribly desolate: it looked as though God was against her. But we shouldn't condemn Naomi just because we know it all worked out right for her in the end. We all go through times when we misunderstand what is happening.

Bitterness separates us from God

People often feel they can excuse themselves if they become bitter over unjust circumstances. But the reality is that we're in the hands of a Father who is kind and just. Psalm 145:17 says, 'The Lord is righteous [just] in all his ways and loving towards all he has made.' Bitterness is a symptom of a lack of faith in God's goodness. When we succumb to it, our relationship with him dries up. Lack of faith robs us of our enjoyment of God.

If we can see that our disappointments are God's appointments, then we can say, 'Lord, I don't understand what's happening to me, but I know something good will come out of it.' What God really wants, as 1 Corinthians 7:35 says, is to secure our 'undivided devotion'. Psalm 86:11 says, 'Give me an undivided heart that I may fear your name.' God's desire has always been for a relationship with his people; he wants us to love him—heart, mind, soul and strength. God knows that a relationship with him is the most deeply satisfying thing we can ever experience. Hence, if we're single, we are to be devoted to him. If we're married, we are to be devoted to him. If we are widowed, we are to be devoted to him. It's so easy to get earthbound in our thinking. Marriage is a precious thing, but it's an earthly relationship. The relationship we have with God is eternal. There will be no marrying in heaven. There, we won't be saying, 'I wish I'd been married on earth because I'm losing out now.' No, what matters most, today and for eternity, is our relationship with God.

When we dwell on the disappointments in our lives—'I'm not married' or 'I'm not being used'—we rob ourselves of life's most valuable possession. If we focus on what God really wants, then we won't miss anything. God wants to use our disappointments to cause us to go deeper in our relationships with him. He wants us to discover, in the midst of adversity, the heights and depths of his love, grace, mercy and kindness. God wants us to understand that he is the answer to our needs. The situation we're disappointed about could be the very thing that is robbing us of that very special relationship with him.

Be alert to the danger of bitterness. It invariably affects the people close to us. Our pessimism sours their attitudes, and the poison keeps spreading, with devastating results. See to it, Hebrews 12:15 says, that no bitter root grows up in you to cause trouble and defile many. There's only one way of escape: repent of a wrong attitude, cry out to God for his forgiveness, and receive his love afresh.

Honest about feelings

When she arrived in Bethlehem, Naomi told the women to call her Mara, 'bitter', because 'The Almighty has made my life very bitter.' Indeed, God had allowed Naomi to suffer great loss. I believe she was just being very honest and human. She was grieving for her sons and her husband, who had died in a foreign land. No wonder the outlook was discouraging. We must never be afraid to face reality and just 'tell it like it is'. As a new widow, if I would have told my friends 'Life is fantastic!' that would have been superspiritual hypocrisy. We need friendships in which we can be truthful with each other and not have to keep up a false front.

I find it impossible to believe, as some commentators suggest, that Naomi had become a bitter old woman. Though Naomi believed the Lord had brought suffering into her life, she hadn't abandoned her faith. She still saw God's hand on her life. What young woman would choose to spend the rest of her days with a sour-faced mother-in-law? It's noteworthy, too, that the people in Bethlehem didn't start calling Naomi by the name Mara, bitter. I think it just didn't fit.

Ruth, like Naomi, was also going through a difficult time. Her marriage had ended in sorrow. What did life have to offer her? She was faced with one of the most difficult decisions of her life: to go with Naomi or stay with her family in Moab. Staying put her in danger of relinquishing the faith that had been growing in her heart. However, she would more likely find another husband among her own people. By leaving, she would sacrifice her best chance of fulfilling her desire for marriage and motherhood. The choice she made required courage and faith: she would follow Naomi on a hazardous journey to a strange land where she faced an uncertain future. Ruth's decision speaks volumes about Naomi's character.

Ruth acted as she did because of what she saw in Naomi. Far from being too old and having nothing to offer, Naomi was in her prime, a mature woman. All she had gone through equipped her for the most fruitful phase of her life.

No sudden optimism

When Ruth said she would go with her, Naomi didn't just suddenly pull herself together. Nowhere does the story say that Naomi apologised to Ruth for being so unspiritual. She didn't put on a brave face and exclaim, 'Praise God! Life will be marvellous. I'm trusting God for abundant provision. We'll find a beautiful home in Israel where we can have a great time together.' On the contrary, Naomi was still at rock bottom and unable to lift herself up; yet Ruth still wanted to go with her.

I find that example most encouraging. We are never too feeble to demonstrate the grace of God to others. People feel comfortable being with those who are not too proud to reveal their weaknesses as well as their successes. We can share the lessons we've learned from our mistakes. As long as we're following the Lord whole-heartedly and still learning, we only have to be one step ahead to be worth following! 'When I am weak, then I'm strong,' Paul said. He made it clear that his strength was gained through difficulties, insults, hardships and persecution (2 Cor 12:9–10). The grace of God has to be experienced in the school of life.

An onlooking world needs to see people who have found a relationship with God that not only gives them great joy and security, but enables them to come through sorrow and hardship without being shaken. That's how our neighbours and workmates will be drawn to Christ. Ruth was attracted to the Lord by an older woman whom she had observed closely. What she saw made her long to have the same experience.

Naomi was not a worn-out possession to be put on the shelf and eventually discarded. God had much more for her to do. Now she had a young companion whose freshness and courage inspired her as they made their way together to Bethlehem. Ruth had made a difficult decision, but there's always a sense of peace and fulfilment when you know you've made the right choice. Choosing to go God's way never results in loss; it always results in blessing.

Bible Study: Getting a new perspective

For a while, Naomi lost her perspective. She felt discouraged, useless, 'on the shelf'. A faulty perspective will make us prey to the same discouragement.

Nothing in Scripture supports the notion that life will dry up as we advance in years. Many of our unrealised dreams are shadows compared to the real purpose God has for our lives. By focusing our

attention on our unfulfilled hopes, we rob ourselves
of the joy God has for us now. So let's look at how
we can change focus and gain a new perspective.

1. The first thing to do is to take our eyes off ourselves and fix our gaze firmly on Jesus. Read
Hebrews 12:1–2 and Galatians 2:20.

2. We are in a good position to overcome our weaknesses when we rely on God's strength. Paul was a
mighty apostle, yet he learned this lesson. Read 2
Corinthians 12:7–10. What do you think Paul meant
by 'weakness'? What is it that enables us to be
strong?

3. How one serves God will vary according to age,
ability and experience. When we look at other
people who appear more successful than ourselves,
we often end up thoroughly discontented. That attitude needs to be changed. What are some wrong
attitudes? Look at 1 Corinthians 12, for example.

4. Discover how these people served the purpose of
God: Stephen (see Acts 6:2–3); Dorcas (Acts 9:39);
Tychicus (Col 4:7–8); Philemon (Philem vv 7,22);
Mary, the mother of James and Salome (Mk 15:40–
41); widows (1 Tim 5:9–10).

Whatever you work at, do it with all your heart,
as working for the Lord, not men (Col 3:17). This
passage puts a new perspective on the labour of our
hands and sets us free from feeling useless.

5. Make a list of all the tasks you do in your everyday life, whether you're working at home or on a
job. Take fresh stock of what you're doing. Tell
yourself, 'I'm doing this for the Lord.' You might
even compose your list by writing, 'I'm washing
nappies for the Lord,' or, 'I'm wiping tables for the

Lord.' Thank God that you have an opportunity to serve him and ask him to give you a new perspective, that you might 'work as unto the Lord'.

6

Look Out! You're Being Followed

> But Ruth replied, 'Don't urge me to leave you or to turn back from you. Where you go I will go, and where you stay I will stay. Your people will be my people and your God my God. Where you die I will die, and there I will be buried. May the Lord deal with me, be it ever so severely, if anything but death separates you and me (Ruth 1:16–18).

Driving down the road one day, I saw a little girl lagging far behind her friend and struggling very hard to keep up. By the way she walked, my first thought was that she was disabled. She could not have been more than five years old, and a pang of pity pierced my heart. Then, as the reason for her strange gait dawned upon me, I burst out laughing. She was wearing a pair of ridiculously large high-heeled shoes, probably her mother's or big sister's! No wonder her friend was way ahead of her.

Children are born with a natural instinct to copy those around them. What great fun to dress up in old clothes, raid Mum's jewel box when she isn't looking, or gyrate in front of a mirror with an imaginary microphone in your hand, singing to thousands of adoring fans!

Watching children imitate adults is amusing, but as they get older it can also produce anxiety as we see the heroes our teens choose to follow. It brings great joy, though, when our prayers are answered and they find the greatest hero of all, responding to his call to 'Follow me.' I was fifteen when I committed my life to Jesus Christ, and my tastes changed dramatically. Down from my bedroom walls came the photos of my favourite film stars. Instead, I began collecting all the books I could find that would help me live for Jesus. My heart was captured, and the power of my new affection dominated my life.

We usually remember those who most influenced us in our spiritual infancy and how we tried to imitate them. I have already mentioned my friend, Mollie, who led me to the Lord at a young age. Her opinions, tastes and lifestyle really mattered to me. I also devoured biographies of people like Hudson Taylor, founder of the China Inland Mission; George Muller and Mary Slessor; and John and Betty Stam, who were martyred during the Boxer uprising in China in 1900, as well as books on the deeper life by Oswald Chambers and Andrew Murray. I wanted to follow in their footsteps and do similar exploits for God.

When I met my future husband, an even more powerful influence was at work. No other human being could exert a greater pull on me. From then on, he was the one I would follow; his opinions counted above all others. Since he was determined to seek the Lord wholeheartedly, I was walking on a sure path.

For many years, the possibility that I was influencing people never occurred to me. I assumed that the only people who were looked to as examples were the 'big shots', spiritual giants like my husband, and men and women who were often in the public eye. When people first began to tell me that something I had said or done had actually affected their lives, I reacted with a mixture of amazement and horror. Then it dawned on me that there are lots of little girls trying to walk in a big person's shoes. Whether we know it or not, those of us who are older are influencing others by the way we live. We are being followed.

Ruth told Naomi she would follow her to her death. That's not something one says lightly. There must have been something special about Naomi for Ruth to have had such confidence in her. Ruth was no child. She was a mature young woman well able to decide for herself what kind of life she wanted. Yet here she was, telling her mother-in-law, of all people, that she would follow her wherever she wanted to go!

The Bible is silent on how Naomi got on with her two daughters-in-law before their husbands died. But it's logical to assume that Naomi's life had come under their close scrutiny. Naomi had spent several years with these women, forming strong bonds of affection. Now the fruit of these relationships became apparent. Though unaware of it, Naomi had been setting a pattern for the women in her family to follow.

The influence of the latest trendsetters in the fashion business is enormous, especially if the designer has a few famous patrons. We might not consider ourselves trendsetters, but if only one person follows our example, the repercussions can continue for eternity. That was true for Naomi—why not for you or me?

I think of Susannah Wesley, born in 1669. A godly woman and devoted mother, Susannah made time for each of her nineteen children, giving each of them an hour of religious instruction each week. Susannah had a great influence on her family, and two of her sons went on to become instrumental in turning the spiritual tide in England during the 1700s: Charles became a famous hymn-writer, and John—her fifteenth child—became a famous evangelist. He rode throughout England, boldly preaching in the open air. His tireless zeal helped spark a great revival in England and led to the foundation of the Methodist Church.

We go along, day by day, never knowing how much impact our actions have on other people. As she spent that weekly hour with each of her children, Susannah Wesley had no idea she was raising one of England's greatest revival teams. Likewise, Naomi never knew how her actions would ripple through the generations that followed. She saw her influence on Ruth's life and the happy marriage to Boaz that followed, but didn't live to see Ruth's great-grandson, David, become the king of Israel. She didn't realise she would be in the lineage of the Messiah. Nor did she have any inkling that her life story would be preserved in Scripture and inspire thousands, centuries after her death.

The relationship challenge

Naomi's influence had much to do with the fact that she succeeded in an important, often hazard-ridden area: relationships. The butt of many stupid jokes, mothers-in-law are often portrayed as possessive and interfering. They are the young bride's nightmare and biggest source of tension. Yet in Naomi we have a mother-in-law to whom Ruth turned in her hour of need. When you're hurting or facing trials, you look to someone you trust, someone with whom you have a secure, loving relationship.

Naomi had to make the adjustments necessary when her son's affection was given to another woman. Genesis 2:24 says that a man leaves his father and mother and cleaves to his wife. Clearly stated, this simple principle forms the basis of good relationships. Parents, don't be anxious when your sons and daughters cut the apron strings; lovingly let them go. When a new home is being set up, God desires the husband to be head of that household. It's important to respect his authority and not try to impose your superior wisdom on him.

By adopting a good attitude, we can build wonderful, lasting relationships with our in-laws and in no sense ever 'lose' our children. It's great to be able to enjoy a new son or daughter added to the family by marriage. Sadly, these are relationships in which even Christians can fail miserably. Love never fails, but sometimes, however hard we try, our efforts seem to be of no avail. That's when it's vital to pray for grace and patience to keep working at it. Those who are older and more mature are responsible for being the peacemakers.

One of Arthur's favourite sayings was, 'The

church is not buildings, but relationships.' The
church is a family where relationships are worked
out in everyday living as we rub shoulders with one
another. Jesus said, 'All men will know that you are
my disciples if you love one another' (Jn 13:35).
Children attain their full potential in a family
atmosphere in which love prevails. It's the same in
church: 'babes' in Christ grow best in the security
of a loving environment.

How do we rate in our relationships? Are we
over-sensitive, critical, always reacting to others'
mistakes, grumblers, tale-bearers? Or are we ready
to be friends? Are we on the lookout for lonely
people too shy to express their need for someone to
talk to? Reaching out to others is something we can
all do to build the church. Loving people is a ministry without a label, but it holds everything else
together. Above all, Colossians 3:14 says, we should
put on love, which binds everything together in
perfect harmony.

Walking in a different direction

Ruth looked on Naomi as a mentor, someone who
would teach her how to 'walk' in a new way. The
Scriptures offer plenty of instruction about how
God's children are to walk in order to be worth
following. For one, we're not to conform to the
world, which means that we sometimes have to lead
out and walk in a direction that's different from that
of the crowd.

As a teenager, I hated to be different. I didn't
want to stand out; it was far more comfortable to be
one of the crowd. But when I came to know Jesus, I

had to make a choice about how I was going to live. I recall one small issue, in particular, that became a big victory. I often took the bus to a Christian meeting and always brought my Bible along. I remember how important I felt it was to carry my Bible openly in my hand and not hide it in a bag. I thought the decision cost me a lot. I was convinced the other passengers were gazing at my Bible and thinking I was a religious nut!

We're called to proclaim Jesus as the way, the truth and the life. But what does that mean? It means that by the way we live we're to stand out in stark contrast to the darkness around us. We're to be 'blameless and pure, children of God without fault in a crooked and depraved generation, in which you shine like stars in the universe' (Phil 2:15). That challenge will require us to make much bigger choices than just being seen with a Bible.

Together with thousands of other Christians, early this year I attended a meeting in the Albert Hall, London. We had come to express our unanimous concern about the rising number of abortions in our nation, to pray and to support the valiant efforts of Christian Members of Parliament, of doctors and others to bring about a change. As we entered the building we ran the gauntlet of shouted abuse from a column of men and women marching round the hall. Later, during the meeting, the speakers were interrupted by further shouting, and I believe the police had to make some arrests. One senior MP was even assaulted in the street after he left the meeting.

This experience brought home to me that we are already in an era of violent protest and lawlessness.

It is time to stand up and be counted, unafraid but knowing that in the strength of the Lord and clothed in his armour we will overcome.

Womanhood is under attack in our society. The younger generation needs our support to help resist the onslaught of a permissive society. For one, let us uphold without compromise the sanctity of marriage, and the beauty of sexual relationships as God intended, only within marriage. Likewise, in other questions of morality we must hold fast to God's word, for any other way will only bring sorrow.

Instructions on walking

Our words and actions—the way we 'walk'— reveal what's in our hearts. Those of us who are mature are called to be totally devoted to Christ and his kingdom and to let our walk with God be an example for others. Throughout Scripture, the words 'walk' and 'life' are used interchangeably. Note these instructions:

- Walk humbly with your God (Mic 6:8)
- Walk in newness of life (Rom 6:4)
- Walk by faith (2 Cor 5:7)
- Walk in the Spirit (Gal 5:16)
- Walk in a manner worthy of our high calling (Eph 4:1)
- Walk carefully (Eph 5:15)
- Walk in the light as children of light (Eph 5:8; 1 Jn 1:7).

John's first epistle (2:6) sums it all up for us: 'Walk as Jesus did.' This might sound like an impossible goal, but the good news is that Jesus broke the barriers when he died on the cross.

Through Jesus, we can now choose to walk in new-ness of life. The grace of God will teach us how to say no to temptation and to live to please our Father (Tit 2:11–12). Notice the word 'teach'. God needs to teach us because we have a lot to learn. I find that encouraging. We don't have to be perfect before we're worth following. As long as we respond to the grace of God and keep on learning, we can set an example for others who are learning, too.

Naomi didn't have a crowd of admiring fol-lowers. She had two young women, only one of whom stuck with her to the end. But her influence on that one person caused the last years of her life— when she thought she was too old to be of any use—to be fruitful far beyond her wildest dreams!

We all have an influence on someone, whether good or bad, though we're often unaware of it. A girl recently came up to me and said boldly, 'When I grow up, I want to be like you.' In addition to being a lovely compliment, the comment came as quite a shock because I hardly knew this girl. Though we rarely tell those whom we're trying to emulate, we all look to other people as role models. Let your prayer be, 'Lord, make me someone who sets an example you want others to follow.'

Bible Study: Keep walking

Pat Goldring, a dear friend of mine, was confined to a wheelchair after having both her legs amputated late in life. In spite of days when she went through deep depression and loneliness, she walked with Jesus until the day he took her to be with himself. Though she felt useless in her handicap, her friends saw her in a different light. They had a deep appreciation for her gift for story-telling, her sense of humour and her artistic abilities.

A sister-in-law who spent many hours caring for this woman, came to the Lord through her quiet testimony. She saw Jesus in her by the way she coped with her difficulties. Pat wrote letters to influential people, company directors, well known personalities and even the nobility. She told them about the research carried out by the professor in St Bartholemew's Hospital, London, whose skill had saved her life, asking for their support. Thousands of pounds were donated in response. In gratitude the hospital authorities invited Pat to meet Princess Alexandra when she visited the hospital and also named a room after Pat.

Pat's life demonstrated what walking with God is all about—just being an ordinary woman following Jesus through the ups and downs of life.

Begin this study by reading and discussing the verses cited in this chapter referring to our 'walk'. That subject is too big to cover fully in one short study, but you can share a few encouraging thoughts.

You may want to study the subject later in more depth, either as a group or individually. When you have time, take a concordance and as many versions of the Bible as you have and write down references to the word 'walk' along with any appropriate comments. You don't have to do it all in one sitting; you can add to your list every time you come across another verse.

Don't worry about things in the Bible that puzzle you. It is better to feed on what you do understand than to get bogged down with too many questions. God has a way of clearing the mist and doubt just when we really need to know. Meanwhile, here are some hints to help you in your walk.

1. Help is at hand. Read Psalm 37:23–24 and Jude 24.

2. How to know the way. Read Psalm 119:105.

3. We can help each other. Read Ecclesiastes 4:9–10, Romans 1:11–12, Proverbs 27:5–6 and Ephesians 6:18–19.

4. Our source of strength. Read Hebrews 4:16, Romans 6:14 and Philippians 4:13.

5. How is it really possible to walk as Jesus walked? Read Galatians 2:20 and 2 Peter 1:3–4.

7

There's No Place Like Home

So the two women went on until they came to Bethlehem (Ruth 1:19).

Home sweet home! The word 'home' stirs some
warm emotions, doesn't it? The fond feelings
associated with it have inspired artists, musicians
and poets through the centuries to produce some of
their most captivating creations.

I've had the opportunity to see a great variety of
homes throughout the world. While visiting
Harewood House in Yorkshire, a centuries-old
estate belonging to relatives of the royal family, I
developed a crick in my neck as I gazed at the high
ceilings. They were elaborately carved, painted
with brilliant colours, and hung with sparkling
chandeliers. In each room, the recorded voice of the
Earl of Harewood described the furnishings, making me feel as though he were personally escorting
me through his home. The surrounding grounds,
designed by a renowned landscape architect, were
breathtaking, laid out with acres of lakes, terraces
and beautiful flower gardens.

On another occasion, I marvelled at a colourful

collection of ornate gypsy caravans. They were like small palaces on wheels; the wood was intricately carved and painted in spectacular hues. The insides were neatly divided into sleeping and cooking areas. Beautiful silks and cushions adorned the beds, and the cupboards were decorated in beautiful patterns of gold and blue. The detailed craftsmanship and superb colours took my breath away.

Once, on a trip to Bombay, next to luxury high-rise hotels, I saw makeshift tents that represented the only home thousands of poor people knew. Some slept on the pavement. One family lived in a huge concrete pipe. My heart longed to move them into something that could justifiably be called home.

What is a home?

What is it that first comes to mind when you think of home? Is it the building itself? Perhaps it's the image of being curled up by the fire, absorbed in a good book; perhaps the aroma of your favourite food wafting from the kitchen is for you the essence of home. Or perhaps it's your own room: the view from the window, the sight of a cherished possession. Home causes us to recall many images, many memories.

Some homes I've stayed in were elegantly furnished; others were simple but comfortable; some were spartan, lacking all but the barest necessities. But whether you live in a cardboard shack, a gypsy caravan, or a sprawling mansion, the structure itself does not constitute 'home', nor the lack of it. Home is not primarily a building or the possessions it holds. You can live in a beautiful house, but if you don't feel comfortable with the people living there, you won't feel 'at home'. Home has to do with people. It's being at home with people you love and knowing the security of their presence. For Ruth, home was wherever Naomi was.

Turning a house into a home

Homemaking is a gift that many women naturally possess, but it's a gift we can all acquire, single and married women alike, if we value it highly. Some women are naturally good at looking after a home, organising it, and making it attractive. Skills such as these can be learned and improved. But a real homemaker is someone whose heart is directed towards other people, not towards herself.

If you have a heart that's concerned about other people, your concern will be expressed in your home. You will make people feel accepted and valued. This personal care and attention shouldn't just be directed towards visitors, though; the family deserves more than leftovers. The home is for those who live there permanently. If you care for your family first, they will want to be caring towards others. When your family members are secure and happy, then you can provide a home that others will be glad to visit.

A homemaker should try to create an atmosphere in which people feel at ease and free to be themselves. Most people don't feel at home if they're treated as special guests and never allowed to come into the kitchen to wash up alongside the host or hostess. I had to learn this lesson myself. Early in my married life, guests would ask me, 'Is there anything I can do to help?' I would always say, 'Oh, no. Just relax.' But then I'd feel under pressure to get all the work done and be worn out from doing everything myself. When I allowed guests to help, they felt more at home, and we were all more relaxed.

Of course, times of tension in family life are bound to occur. Upheavals and squabbles occur in every household, but peace will prevail if there's a sense that Jesus is present and there is a readiness to forgive. Ruth had tasted the warmth, peace and security of her mother-in-law's home; this no doubt helped convince her to stay with Naomi.

It's interesting that Ruth didn't wait to see what kind of place Naomi settled in before deciding whether or not to live with her. Ruth had no idea what type of accommodation might await her in Israel. Presumably, Naomi's old dwelling would either have been sold, taken over by another family, or left unoccupied, in which case it might well have been uninhabitable. Setting out for Israel without a home awaiting them must have been a step of faith for both women, but Naomi herself represented home to Ruth, and Ruth could think of no better place to be than with her.

One can imagine Ruth, as she and Naomi travelled, asking all sorts of questions about life in Bethlehem and wondering how she would be received. The prospect of setting up a new home must have given her a mixture of excitement and apprehension. Naomi's assurances, though, would have been an anchor in a sea of uncertainty.

A privilege

What a privilege it is to be a homemaker, especially if you have a home of your own. Once I had recovered from the initial shock of losing my husband, I felt immensely grateful to my heavenly Father for providing me with the house into which we had just moved. It is so right for me at this stage of life. There is ample room for entertaining guests, so I prayed that God would 'people' my house! Nice as it was to visit friends and be a guest, I longed for company in my own home. God answered that prayer when he knew I was capable of coping with it, and it has been a joy to exercise the gift of hospitality once more. Just as I was writing this chapter, a photo arrived in the post. 'I thought you would like this picture of your home,' the sender wrote. 'It was a joy to stay with you.'

We can all use our homes to serve the Lord, whether 'home' is a forty-room mansion or a tiny room in a basement. You don't have to be married to be a homemaker, either. Jesus loved to go to the home of three single people who lived together: Lazarus and his two sisters, Martha and Mary (Jn 11:5). Jesus found something very attractive about their home. It wasn't because their house was particularly splendid or because the location was a convenient walk from Jerusalem. He just enjoyed being with the people who lived there. When he was there, they made him feel at home.

How did this come about? Very simply. The Bible says Martha opened her home to Jesus, and he came in (Lk 10:38). What kind of a home was it? Well, Martha was a woman who loved to serve. Nothing pleased her more than providing a tasty meal and inviting guests to share it. The trouble was that she tended to overdo things and wear herself out working so hard to please, especially when Jesus arrived. So at times the atmosphere became a bit tense in the kitchen and threatened to spill over into the rest of the house. She had yet to learn that Jesus loved her for herself, not for the meals she prepared for him. All her hard work was preventing him from enjoying her presence.

Inviting Jesus into her home taught Martha an important lesson; one every aspiring homemaker ought to learn. If we are so weary from preparing meals and performing household chores that we have no time to sit and enjoy guests, they will feel unwelcome and burdensome. The problem can often be solved with simpler meals and less fuss when time is limited. We create an atmosphere of peace when we are at peace. I don't think it could have been long before Martha learned this lesson, with Jesus there to teach her and with her sister's example.

Mary was different from her sister. She loved to sit and listen to people talk, especially when Jesus came in. When her household gave a dinner in Jesus' honour, Mary extravagantly poured out her perfume on Jesus' feet, thus filling her house with a lovely fragrance (Jn 12:3). This was a spontaneous act of worship. In a home where Jesus is central to family life, it's quite natural for the occupants to burst into songs of praise.

Martha and Mary's household had every reason to rejoice. The reason Jesus was the guest of honour was because he had raised Lazarus from the dead. God had chosen Lazarus to be the proof of Jesus' authority over death (Jn 11:25–26). Their home would never be the same. People came to hear all about the miracle and the man who performed it. This home became a place of testimony, a place where seekers could find the truth, a place where Christ was proclaimed, and many came to believe in him. Isn't that what we want in our homes? Each time Arthur and I moved into a new house, we knelt on the first day and prayed that God would use our home as a place where people could meet with Jesus.

A home open to Jesus brings many opportunities for serving the Lord. One time we had a couple over who were looking for a church to link themselves with. We had tea, and afterwards, as we often did, we talked about the Lord and prayed together. At one point, the man suddenly said, 'Right. This is it.'

'What do you mean?' we asked.

'This is church,' he said. 'This is where we want to come. Let's come again next week.' That was the beginning of a church that met in our house for two or three years before it outgrew that setting and moved into a building. Our home was also the site for several years of monthly prayer meetings, in which we would gather to pray for revival.

It was at home that we also began a missionary supply service as a way of helping people who were labouring for the gospel in difficult conditions overseas. This project started when we asked about a dozen missionaries we knew if they would like to receive cassette tapes and goods that were scarce or very expensive on the mission field. The response was positive, so we began sending parcels. We gradually learned what items were most suitable

and began enclosing a checklist of what we could
supply, asking missionaries to choose items they
found most valuable.

Volunteers from our church would regularly
gather in our home to pack boxes with such items as
vitamin tablets, dried baby foods that could be
stored without refrigeration, freeze-dried meals,
drink concentrates, tins of meat, dried vegetables
and soups, soap, toothpaste and toothbrushes, cake
mixes and sweets for children. Along with food and
household goods, we sent Christian books, mes-
sages that we recorded at churches and conferences,
and a regular newsletter offering encouragement
and news of what God was doing in Britain.

We never advertised Supply Line or sought to
increase it. We just let God bring us the people he
wanted to bless; in that way we never went beyond
our capability. We could easily have been overwhelmed if we had advertised. Hence, as the undertaking grew over the years, we were able to handle
the increase. To keep up with the workload, a full-
time secretary was needed. A missionary who had
herself been on the receiving end of the ministry
came back to England just at the right time to help
us. Eventually we were assisting more than 600
missionaries from 70 mission fields on nearly every
continent of the world. The entire work was run
from our home.

Many of these missionary friends visited us, of
course, while on furlough, and through the years
we had countless overnight guests—missionaries
as well as friends, strangers, foreign visitors, pastors and others in ministry. One night we had
people sleeping on the beds and floors of almost

every room in the house except the kitchen and bathroom.

Through the years, we nearly always had some-body living in our house with us. Often an individual would stay for several weeks or months. One woman had been through a divorce; another had suffered a nervous breakdown. Once we opened our home to a boy whose parents had moved and who wanted to finish the year at the local school. He stayed with us during the week and went home at weekends.

It was enjoyable extending help and getting to know these people, whether through talking over a problem or a situation, praying together, or sharing a scripture. You don't always know what impact you will have on someone. A conversation around the dinner table may have life-changing con-sequences for someone God happens to bring in. Some of our guests needed counsel; others just needed a break from the rush of life to hear what God was saying about their lives and future. These were not one-sided relationships. I learned so much; they were a great blessing to us.

The early church met in homes, and many churches today are still finding the home an ideal setting for fellowship and evangelism. No one with a home ever needs to feel useless in the service of Christ.

Knitting of hearts

Arthur and I also appreciated the kindness of Chris-tians who gave us loving hospitality. We had the privilege of staying in many homes and we

developed a link with many families. We really felt
'at home' and refreshed, and often returned to those
places.

One couple we grew close to were house group
leaders in a church in Maryland where Arthur often
spoke. They made us feel welcome and appreciated,
often serving us American treats that we didn't
have at home. One day we arrived on Arthur's
birthday. Somehow the couple had found out about
it and made a cake for him, complete with candles
and a round of 'Happy Birthday'. They also had the
opportunity to come and stay with us in England.
These people gave themselves to us, and we had a
lot of fun together. Arthur used to tease Liz about
her Virginia accent, and she got a big kick out of it.
She and her husband were hungry for God, and it
was refreshing to be with them. Their home had a
gentle, peaceful atmosphere, making it obvious that
Jesus was at the centre. After Arthur died, I spent a
few days with them, and it was a comfort to be
there. When their third child was born, they named
him Peter Arthur in memory of Arthur.

Paul had a home to which he would invite himself whenever he felt the need to recover his
strength. It belonged to Philemon, and it was a
place of love, joy and refreshment to Paul, as well as
a house of prayer (Philem 7,22). People delight to
stay in a house of prayer, a place where it is natural
to talk to our heavenly Father about everything, a
place where we can be spiritually natural and naturally spiritual. In a home where people pray, Jesus
takes the central place.

Travelling to a new home

In Moab Naomi had made a home in which people prayed to the one true God. Surely she and Ruth prayed for safe travel on a journey that would take them through an area where bandits often robbed and killed their victims. Perhaps they were able to join a caravan of camels conveying travellers and goods to Bethlehem. Such a journey sounds romantic, but much of it was through the barren desert around the Dead Sea. Beyond the Jordan River, though, the desolate terrain gave way to the verdant hills and valleys of Israel. Ruth was coming to a land of much greater beauty than Moab, and her heart must have filled with fresh hope.

How Ruth and Naomi must have looked forward to settling into a home once again. We're not told what particular skills Naomi, a lifelong homemaker, might have passed on to her daughter-in-law. Was she artistic and creative with her hands? Could she weave beautiful wall hangings and mats for the floors? Did she love flowers and decorate her home with the flowers of the field? Perhaps Ruth and Orpah had been skilled in the crafts of their own nation. Back in Moab, the three probably exchanged recipes and helped each other decorate their homes, just as women do today.

There is much that older women can share about creativity in the home. The availability of convenience foods and ready-made meals has robbed us of the need to provide good home cooking for our families. I still love making my own jam and never cease savouring that moment of pride when I turn out homemade bread to cool on the rack.

Of course, time doesn't always permit home

cooking, and there's no need to feel guilty. I can recall the era when women considered anything that wasn't made from basic ingredients a failure. In the early days of my marriage, I made absolutely everything from scratch for the sake of economy and for the pleasure in the achievement. But at times I became like Martha and wore myself out. My pride was blooming. It grew every time anyone complimented me on the food, and I could say I had made it all myself. God had to teach me some lessons on humility. My pride in my kitchen achievements had finally been buried once and for all when I learned to accept a dish or two from invited guests and then hear them get the commendations! I had to learn that time is a valuable commodity in the service of Christ and that it was better to run to the shops to buy a cake than to be worn out from making one.

Teaching by example

Paul urged Titus to let the older women teach the younger women. Those who are spiritually mature and have lived long enough to gain experience have something to share. I have listened to some excellent Bible studies on the second chapter of Titus, which sets forth principles of life for the Christian woman. But not many of us are gifted to teach like that. I doubt whether Naomi invited Ruth and Orpah to her home for a weekly study on the art of homemaking. She probably just let her daughters-in-law observe the way she handled her household and offered help when it was needed.

When an older woman befriends a younger one,

she can serve as a godly mentor, providing invaluable one-to-one instruction. Some of us are too proud to admit we need help, but that shows a lack of wisdom. The wise are always ready to learn; it's only the foolish who won't listen (Prov 19:20). Sharing our own mistakes and how we learned from them will be a far more effective teaching technique, however, than merely pointing out all the things the other person is doing wrong!

A friend of mine, a leader's wife with a busy household to manage, was floundering after the birth of a new baby. Keeping house was a pressure on her because it wasn't her natural gift. Moreover, as a leader, she felt she ought to do better. God used a bout of flu to resolve the difficulty. While my friend was laid up, a young woman offered to help. She was only a young convert, but she was marvellous in the home and soon had everything running smoothly. These two women eventually became good friends and began to help each other. The young woman was full of questions about the Scriptures and eager to learn everything she could. My friend loved studying the Bible and was never happier than when she could give herself to it. So they began getting together both to study the Bible and to help my friend learn how to do household tasks more efficiently. Each encouraged the other. If the leader's wife had been too proud to be helped, she would never have had the joy of influencing a young woman spiritually. I can personally testify that along the way she has learned to be a very good homemaker.

Those of us who are older set a pattern for the younger women to follow, but we teach more often by example than by specific instruction. Pray for the opportunity to influence others in your home, yet also be willing to learn from them. Aim to create a real home, a home where there is a sense of peace, a home where people will feel welcome, refreshed and stimulated, a home where conversation is not all small talk but where people seek to encourage one another in the Lord. Create this kind of home and then share it with others. Hospitality is not a burden; it's not something wearying to dread. Enjoy it! By seizing the opportunity to make your house a real home for people, you will find yourself on a new path of fulfilling service.

Bible Study: A fresh look at the home

As a young wife, I rejected the advice someone once gave me that a woman's place is in the home. After two years of Bible college I considered myself trained and was eager to serve God. In no way was I going to 'vegetate' at home! I had the mistaken idea, however, that my service for the Lord was only what I did in addition to being a wife, mother and homemaker. My attitude needed to change.

Financial and other pressures today encourage women to get out of the home and pursue a 'worthwhile' career. The subtle implication, though, is that homemaking is not so worthwhile. Working outside the home is an individual choice, but beware of the trap of undervaluing a homemaker's role. Perhaps you need a change of attitude, as I did.
1. What does 1 Timothy 3:1–13 teach us about Paul's thoughts on the home? This passage could be described as his curriculum for leadership training.

What 'college' does he recommend, one that will
produce the best graduates? (See vv 4 and 12.)
2. Women are included in this passage. Write down
all the qualifications required for being 'worthy of
respect'. Don't forget to include those applicable to
both men and women.
3. Would you describe these qualifications as 'gift'
or 'character'? If you are secretly longing to escape
from the rut of 'just being a homemaker', you could
be in danger of missing a golden opportunity to
obtain a first-class degree in this prestigious college
for men and women.

The home life of a career woman or one who is
active in ministry is just as relevant as her outside
activities to the development of her character and to
the effectiveness of her service for God. Attitude is
the key to how well we look after our homes.
4. Discuss the importance of the following, and see
if you can find additional scriptures on these topics.
● The outside appearance of the home (Prov 24:30–
34).
● Orderliness inside (Prov 31:27).
● Hospitality: joy or burden (Heb 13:2; 1 Pet 4:9)?
● Creating the right atmosphere (Prov 17:1).
● Making the home attractive (Eccles 3:11; Ps 96:6).
5. Do you think these things have any bearing on
our witness to Christ? How do they undermine or
enhance our testimony?

8

Good Company

Your people will be my people (Ruth 1:16).

The company we keep says something about us. Neighbours are often very observant, especially about the kind of people who regularly come to our house. When we moved for the first time, we hired a van and several members of our church gave us a hand. It was hard work but a lot of fun. Our new neighbours could not help but observe the young men hauling in the heavy furniture, women turning up with food, and the comings and goings for the next few days as various people assisted us.

A few days later, during a friendly chat over the garden wall, my neighbour commented on how many people had turned up and how happy they seemed. She was most surprised when I told her they were all members of our church. 'What church do you attend?' she asked. She was rather puzzled when I told her we call ourselves The Community Church.

'Tell me what that means,' she said. The conversation eventually led me to tell her what we believed about Jesus and about the need to belong to a church. But I began by explaining that we had chosen our name because we desire to be a community of people. 'We don't just attend services on Sunday, but we express our love and care for one another in practical ways,' I told her. 'We do things like helping people move and offering support in times of trouble. We read in the Bible that that's the way to show we are Jesus' disciples.'

'That's what church ought to be like,' she replied. During the next few years, Arthur and I got to know this woman and her husband as good friends. They met other Christians in our home and were always ready to listen to our testimony, yet without taking that step of faith themselves. When another neighbour told the husband I was to undergo cancer surgery, he expressed concern and offered the comment, 'Eileen will be all right because the people in her church will take good care of her.'

The kind of people we associated with made a deep impression on our neighbours. I would not be surprised to learn some day that this couple has decided to join the church, too.

In the world, but avoiding evil

In the natural course of events, we find ourselves involved with all kinds of people, some good, some evil. Jesus does not call us to shut ourselves off from negative influences, as though we lived in a monastery, but to be salt and light. Many believers are surrounded by people whose outlook, interests, lifestyle and moral standards are totally different from theirs. Sooner or later the differences become apparent. If your life centres on the church, it will greatly contrast with that of one whose activities centre on a particular hobby, sport, or club. Jesus' prayer for us is not that we be taken out of the world, but that we be kept from evil (Jn 17:15). To this end, it's vital that we choose to keep company with the right kind of people. Life is full of choices about those with whom we spend time.

When I became a Christian, I found many new friends, but I also lost some old ones who were not prepared to follow Jesus. Sometimes loved ones and friends we cherish pull us away from a life that really pleases God, and at times we have to make some traumatic decisions. 'Bad company corrupts good character,' says 1 Corinthians 15:33. The decision about how to handle a friendship boils down to what kind of influence that person has on us. Is he or she keeping us from going on with God? Or do we believe that God can bring something good out of the relationship? Decisions about what friendships to pursue and at what level depend on the lifestyle we've lived before coming to the Lord and on our spiritual maturity.

A time of decision

Ruth had come to a place of decision. 'Your people shall be my people,' she told Naomi. It was one thing to follow the ways of Jehovah when Naomi was around, but she knew it would be very difficult to follow the God of Israel if she were on her own among her Moabite relatives.

Ruth's decision had some consequences among her friends and family. I can imagine Ruth's family reproaching her for acting more like an Israelite

than a Moabite. Naturally, she would want to join
in her own family gatherings and maintain some
loving contact with her relatives. But in the midst of
her heathen surroundings, the influence of Naomi
held firm her resolve to live a different life.

Perhaps you remember how hard it was as a babe
in Christ to take up the cross and follow Jesus with a
whole heart. How reassuring it was to confide in an
older Christian who understood your struggle and
could say, 'Yes, I found that hard, too, but God gave
me strength and helped me deal with the consequences.' Older Christians provide the stability
and encouragement that younger believers need.

Of course, we can't encourage others to associate
with the right kind of people if we're not doing so
ourselves. If we're going to be women worth following, by all means we must commit ourselves to a
local church and get involved with the people. It's
important to find a place where we feel at home and
then settle there. Attending a different church each
week to do some 'sermon tasting' provides an artifi-
cial diet and is not conducive to healthy growth in
God.

When making a significant decision about moving for a job change or perhaps choosing which
university to attend, it's important to know that we
will have a church where we can find fellowship
and encouragement, rather than going somewhere
where we'll be isolated. A church is not just a meeting place where we go to 'get fed' once a week. The
church should be a community of believers, as I told
my neighbour—an extended family in which
people's lives are truly joined together. In 1 Corinthians 12 Paul says we are linked to the body of

Christ: if I'm a hand, I need to be connected to the arm to function properly. If we take our proper place, we will be a blessing to other people, and will find fulfilment in blessing them. God has not designed us to be loners; we need other people, and they need us. How can anyone be part of the body of Christ while remaining apart from the church? A piece of coal in the middle of the fire burns brightly. Take it out and it soon dies down. All of us need fellowship with the right people to maintain our 'glow'. That requires more than just attending a Sunday meeting.

In the 1960s thousands of young people were swept into the kingdom of God in Britain, and as a result, a new breed of churches sprang up spontaneously. In these non-denominational churches, which eventually numbered in the hundreds, sometimes dry religious ritual gave way to worship and praise and a genuine excitement for God. When this was just beginning, Arthur and I visited such a church, which like many others of the time was meeting in a home. The group was made up primarily of young people. The leader himself was no more than thirty; Arthur and I were old enough to be his parents. While we were there, a young man in his late teens came up to me and asked, 'Are there many older people like you in our churches?' He was relieved when I assured him that there were others. He said it made him more secure to know that this 'movement' he had become part of wasn't just limited to young people, but that some of life's more seasoned sailors were aboard the ship.

The wisdom and experience of older believers act as an anchor to a church. We are tempted to relax

and take it easy when we get older, but a younger
generation needs us. We will always have a vital
part to play. If you know some 'anchors' in your
church, let them know they are appreciated.

Finding new friends

Ruth was going to a land where she would have to
find new friends. She was prepared to take the risk,
let go of old friendships, and be identified with
those who loved Jehovah. She probably wondered
how many other women she would meet who pos-
sessed the qualities she found so attractive in
Naomi. When I'm travelling, the unexpected opportunities I have to meet and get to know other Christians never cease to encourage me.

Arthur and I were sitting in the departure lounge
at Heathrow Airport once, waiting to board a flight
for the United States. I couldn't help overhearing
snatches of the conversation between two American
ladies near me. 'I'm sure these women are Christians,' I whispered to Arthur. Before I could do
anything, we were called to board, and they disappeared into the line ahead of us.

When the plane had climbed high above the
clouds, I felt an urge to see if I could find those
women among the hundreds of passengers. It
didn't take long, and I quickly struck up a conversation with them, learning that they were returning
from a ministry trip to Sweden. When these enthu-
siastic and uninhibited women discovered who we
were, the rest of the passengers were left in no
doubt about their joy! They had read Arthur's
books, so, of course, they wanted him to come over

and be introduced. Our mutual love for Christ over-
came any hesitation or shyness and spilled over to
the people sitting nearby.

We are part of a worldwide community, linked
with bonds that transcend age, nationality and race.
What a privilege to be part of it. May we never be
ashamed to be identified with the family of God;
and as we grow older, may we motivate others to
say, 'Your people shall be my people.'

Bible Study: God's people

In declaring 'Your people shall be my people,' Ruth
was also saying that she wanted to be one of
Jehovah's people. Let's look at what it means to be
God's people.

1. Read 2 Corinthians 6:14—7:1.

2. Verses 14 and 15 give clear guidance on choosing
the right relationships. How would you explain the
meaning of being 'yoked together'?

3. Look up Matthew 11:29–30 and spend a few minutes quietly meditating on these scriptures. Then
share your thoughts with the others in your group,
or write down the difference between this 'yoke'
and the one to avoid.

4. If you are studying on your own, choose either 2
Corinthians 6:16, beginning from 'As God has said',
or 2 Corinthians 6:18 (or both!) to learn by heart. If
you're in a group, read these verses aloud together.
Make them a declaration of faith as you do so.

5. Natural family likeness is usually very obvious to
people outside the family. As God's people, we
want that to be true for us. In the light of 2

Corinthians 7:1, discuss our part in becoming recognisable to the world in which we live. Ephesians 5:26 suggests something we can do.

9

Learning to Know God

Your God [shall be] my God (Ruth 1:16).

Ruth could not have made such a bold statement without apprehension, even fear. Before she met Naomi, the only god she had known about was Chemosh, the god of the Moabites. Fear of this idol so dominated people that they were prepared to sacrifice children to obtain his favour or appease his wrath. No wonder Ruth was attracted to Naomi's God; what she knew of him through Naomi seemed so different from Chemosh.

But would Jehovah reveal himself to her, someone who didn't belong to his chosen nation? Ruth had already seen that identifying with the people of Israel was essential in getting to know their god. Now she finally put into words the longing of her heart: 'Your God shall be my God.' This was no impulsive decision. With this statement came a vow that sealed a lifelong commitment: 'Where you die I will die.' God heard Ruth's cry, for he is found by all who seek him with a pure heart. Naomi, seeing Ruth's heart and how determined she was, no longer tried to dissuade her from going to Bethlehem.

Struggling for words

It was one of those days when writing didn't come
easily; I was groping for what to write in this chapter. I wanted to communicate that knowing God in
an intimate way is more important than anything
else, regardless of one's age or status. I knew this
was the key to being the kind of woman who exerts
a godly influence on those around her. Yet, as I
fought for words to express this, my spirit was
struggling with the loneliness that comes at times
when I miss Arthur. I desperately wished that he
was there, and longed just to talk with him. 'I'm
feeling discouraged, Lord,' I prayed. 'Please give me
something fresh.' Wondering whether I was the
kind of woman who ought to be writing a book like
this, I had to remind myself that Naomi was discouraged at times, too.

God didn't answer my prayer immediately. I laid
my writing aside to attend to more mundane but
more urgent matters—taking my car to a nearby
garage for repairs on the exhaust system. It was a
pleasant fifteen-minute walk home across the common, the largest of several in Southampton. I have
already recounted my joy at living near that pleasant expanse. Every season has its own attraction,
and that day the leaves were displaying the beautiful golds of early autumn.

Because Arthur and I had gone there often, praying informally as we walked together, it has become
natural for me to talk to my heavenly Father as I
walk. It was a wet, windy day, and the falling leaves
made a slippery carpet for my feet. But I was snug
inside my kagoul and enjoyed the fresh air and
exercise as I admired the autumn hues. During my

conversation with Father, I casually asked if he would help me make some progress with my writing while the car was being repaired.

What, I wondered, had stood out in Ruth's mind as she considered the difference between Chemosh and Jehovah? I could search the Bible and find many scriptures and a wealth of doctrinal evidence demonstrating the superiority of one true God. But Ruth had learned something from her mother-in-law that was enough to convince her without any access to a Bible.

I began meditating on Ruth's words, 'Your God shall be my God.' No startling revelation came, just fresh light on a familiar truth. I realised that in saying these words, Ruth suddenly saw that Naomi's God was real: not some feared imaginary beast set in wood or stone, but someone with whom she could have a relationship; someone who had a personal interest in her. Ruth was announcing that Jehovah was her God, her Creator, her Father, and that she was his daughter, a new and beloved member of his family. Naomi knew this God; she talked about him and assumed he was involved in all the events of her life. That was an intimacy Ruth wanted, too. Nobody would dream of having a relationship like that with Chemosh. He was something to be feared, something to appease. Nothing about him would make someone desire a personal relationship with him. He was a god with sightless eyes and unhearing ears, as Psalm 115:4–7 says:

Their idols are silver and gold, made by the hands of men. They have mouths, but cannot speak, eyes, but they cannot see; they have ears, but cannot hear, noses, but they cannot smell; they have hands, but

cannot feel, feet, but they cannot walk; nor can they
utter a sound with their throats.

Christianity is the only religion that offers a personal relationship with God. No other teaching
offers the intimacy and affection that comes from
being born into God's family and knowing him as
our heavenly Father. Ruth had grown up knowing
only a god created out of the fear and imagination of
men. Now she was coming to know the living,
compassionate God, a personal Being who feels
emotion and understands our joys and sorrows
because he made us like himself.

Ruth was experiencing the delight and peace of
having entered a new relationship with her Creator.
The fact that Naomi felt discouraged and useless at
this point in her life didn't matter. Her God understood, and he was using the situation to bring her
into a new and richer relationship with himself.
Reflecting on these things as I walked home, the
discouragement I had felt lifted.

A woman acquainted with God

Every new day brings a fresh opportunity to get to
know God more. What a wealth of experience the
older ones among us have to share. This spiritual
treasure trove is one of our greatest assets. Arthur
often spoke about an elderly lady he knew who had
many such 'treasures'. Though this woman was
probably in her seventies, she was a great friend to
many younger people, including Arthur. Many of
our friends knew her and spoke about her. She had

a reputation as a woman of prayer, someone with the insight that comes only from hearing God.

Poor health had left this woman housebound, but people often came to her home to tell her their troubles, ask her advice, or simply share news. Invariably she would say, 'Let's talk to Father about it, my dear, and see what he has to say.' Then she would talk to God as an intimate friend. People asked her to pray for them and she would regularly bring their concerns before the Lord.

Rebellious in her younger years, this woman had undergone some dramatic lifestyle changes after she came to know the Lord. She spoke freely about God's dealings with her and how she had learned he is a holy God who demands obedience.

Not everyone experiences that same intimacy with God, yet anyone can. God longs for us to desire him more than anything else. The first and greatest commandment is to love the Lord with all your heart, soul, mind and strength (Mk 12:30). This is not a legalistic demand, but a glorious invitation to enjoy God and enjoy being loved by him.

In these days of instant everything—one-minute meals and two-step solutions—we are in danger of expecting easy answers to all our spiritual needs. Instruction on knowing God cannot be condensed into one chapter of a book or even a series of books. We will keep learning more each day of our lives.

Learning the fear of the Lord

Notice what Proverbs 1:7 says is the beginning of knowledge: the fear of the Lord. Fearing God and knowing him intimately go hand in hand; it's impossible to have one without the other. But surely, some might protest, God wants us to love him, not to be afraid of him! Of course. But how can we really love God without giving him the reverence and awe he deserves? How can we say we love him, yet treat his word lightly? The Bible tells us that God esteems those who are humble in spirit and tremble at his word (Is 66:2).

We all admire that woman of excellence portrayed in Proverbs 31. The list of her achievements is quite staggering. She finds success in everything from buying land and planting a vineyard to making and selling fine linen. Most of us are not endowed with such diverse talents, but we can achieve the same excellence in the things God gives us to do. What's the secret of that success? It's found in verse 30: 'A woman who fears the Lord is to be praised.' Such a woman is worth following.

Paul urged Titus to let the older women teach the younger women (Tit 2:3–4). But he was careful to suggest the qualities these women should possess. He said nothing about gifts or abilities; the women who would be best qualified were those who were 'reverent in the way they live'. In other words, they were women who feared the Lord.

To fear the Lord means that we give God his rightful place in our heart. His will becomes our delight. When we fear the Lord, we will be motivated by a strong desire to please him. This won't be a wearisome burden. God knows when we sincerely seek to know him, and he rewards us with knowledge and understanding:

If you call out for insight and cry aloud for understanding, and if you look for it as for silver and search for it as for hidden treasure, then you will understand the fear of the Lord and find the knowledge of God. For the Lord gives wisdom, and from his mouth comes knowledge and understanding (Prov 2:3–6).

This seeking after God, is it for people who can free themselves from family and job responsibilities and devote hours to prayer and spiritual exercises? Quite the contrary. It's in those very situations, in the midst of the strains and struggles of ordinary life, that we learn the fear of the Lord. Any woman can get to know God, even if her days are filled with responsibilities at work or small children requiring her attention at home and at times she's only got five minutes in the day to read the Bible or pray. If she makes God central in her life, giving him his rightful place, then God will reveal himself and she will get to know him and understand his ways, his character, his heart. Those unexpected intervals of quiet and freedom will become oases not to be missed.

Our feet were placed on the path to knowing God the day we were born again. How much have we progressed? Does the knowledge that our sins have been forgiven bring us joy? Does our heart fill with gratitude when we remember how much Jesus suffered for us, the agony the sinless Son of God experienced in being made sin? Or have these truths become so familiar that we're in danger of losing our first love and in need of repentance, as was the Ephesian church in Revelation 2:4?

A jealous God

God always desires to have a deeper relationship
with us. He saves us by his grace and then he
causes us to grow in grace and in the knowledge of
his character (2 Pet 3:18). One facet of God's character emphasised in Scripture is that he desires us to
love him with our whole being:

> Fear the Lord your God, worship only him, and make
> your promises in his name alone. Do not worship
> other gods, any of the gods of the peoples around you.
> If you do worship other gods, the Lord's anger will
> come against you like fire and will destroy you com-
> pletely, because the Lord your God, who is present
> with you, tolerates no rivals (Deut 6:13–15, GNB).

He loves us so much that he will tolerate no rivals.
He wants to lavish his love upon us and set us free
from all that would rob us of the richness of our
inheritance in Christ. But he cannot do this if our
hearts are clinging to idols.

An idol is any person, possession, occupation, or
habit that exerts such a hold on us that it prevents
us from following God with our whole heart. Talents and abilities, for instance a beautiful singing
voice or an artistic flair, can become idols. Such
things are not sinful in themselves; it is the grip
something has on our heart that turns it into an
idol. God gives us a choice, just as Joshua did the
Israelites: 'Fear the Lord...throw away the foreign
gods...yield your hearts to the Lord' (Josh 24:14,23).

As a young man, Arthur was an avid tennis
player. But there came a time in his life when he
knew the sport was becoming too important to him.

The hold it had on him was causing him to spend precious time on the tennis court that could have been used in more valuable ways. So Arthur gave up the game. Some years later, when he had grown in the fear of the Lord, he was able to pick it up once more, for it no longer had any hold on him. Arthur missed some tennis matches, but all those years he enjoyed the benefits of giving God his rightful place in his heart and not letting anything crowd him out.

Films and film stars were my idols as a young person. After I was converted, I faced the challenge of giving them up. I knew I had to give up films completely. My heart is completely free from this idolatry now, and I can enjoy the entertainment of a good film without feeling convicted.

The fear of the Lord teaches us to hate evil. 'Be holy, because I am holy,' says 1 Peter 1:15. That means keeping our conscience clear and seeking the assurance of forgiveness whenever we sin. It's all too easy to harbour secret sins—pride, wrong thoughts and attitudes, behaviour that no one sees—without repenting and dealing with the issue. The Holy Spirit will convict us and show us just where we have failed, not to bring condemnation but to release us from sin and restore the joy of fellowship with God.

There will always be young women like Ruth who observe older women and desire to know and fear God in the same way. They will seek out such women, full of questions, eager to learn, and will be encouraged to hear how someone else came through the struggles and temptations they are now facing.

Bible Study: Start searching

If your appetite has been whetted and you're determined to learn more about the fear of the Lord, ask God to teach you. He will. Don't expect it to happen overnight, though. People can look up a long list of scriptures and fill their minds with facts without ever experiencing the fear of the Lord. It's got to be a heart search, not an intellectual exercise.

1. Find an opportunity to be alone and meditate on Psalm 86:11. If you are in a group, spend some time quietly meditating on this verse together and learning it by heart.

2. God always responds when we sincerely seek him. Read and discuss Jeremiah 32:39. Who is it that is going to bring us into this experience? (See also Phil 1:6.)

3. If you would like to study additional scriptures on the fear of the Lord, here are a few to help you start: Psalms 112 and 25:14, Proverbs 8:13, Isaiah 11:2-4 and 33:5-6, Acts 9:31 and Revelation 15:4. Ask the Holy Spirit to enable you to hide these teachings in your heart, not just in your mind.

4. We all appreciate good friends, people in whom we can confide, knowing they will not betray our secrets. God wants us to enjoy his friendship as well. Read Psalm 25:14 and discuss the privilege reserved for those who fear the Lord. What kinds of things do you think the Lord might confide?

5. If you're in a group, discuss what you understand to be the meaning of 'knowing God'. How far have you progressed? Talk about how you've experienced God's dealings in your life and what you have learned as a result. Pray for one another and encourage each other.

10

Everything's Gone Wrong

When they arrived in Bethlehem, the whole town was stirred because of them, and the women exclaimed, 'Can this be Naomi?' 'Don't call me Naomi,' she told them. 'Call me Mara, because the Almighty has made my life very bitter. I went away full, but the Lord has brought me back empty. Why call me Naomi? The Lord has afflicted me; the Almighty has brought misfortune upon me' (Ruth 1:19–21).

At last, much to Naomi's relief, she and Ruth arrived safely in Bethlehem. Exhausted from the long journey and the emotional strain of it all, Naomi probably just wanted to find somewhere quiet to rest before facing all her old friends. But that wasn't to be. Word of her arrival spread quickly, and the weary traveller soon found herself surrounded by a crowd of women full of amazement and curiosity at seeing her back again after so many years.

Their joy and delight turned to embarrassment as Naomi, unable to hide her feelings, pleaded with them to call her Mara, which means bitter. She did not want them to think of her any longer as someone who always escaped difficulties. Life had been far from pleasant in Moab, and as she recalled her years there, she could only think of how everything in life had gone wrong.

Naomi had lost the husband and sons that meant everything to a Hebrew woman; she didn't even have any grandchildren to carry on her family. Yet even in the midst of her despair, God was with her. She didn't recognise it, but God was working in her life. He was guiding her circumstances, shaping her character, teaching her valuable lessons. Everything had a purpose.

When our world seems to fall apart, God doesn't always put the pieces back together as before. Nonetheless, we can trust that he is at work in the situation. As we suffer losses and disappointments, we need to recognise that nothing goes wrong with God. Everything is part of his plan. He is with us in the midst of pain and adversity, just as he was with Naomi, offering us another lesson in his grace and sufficiency. It's a mark of immaturity to see Christianity as a garden of thornless roses; mature Christianity is being able to walk with God through the thorns and to discover how he brings blessing from them as well as from the roses.

Home again

The gloom of ten years before had lifted from Bethlehem. The famine that had threatened the village with starvation had passed, and food was no longer scarce. In fact, Ruth and Naomi's arrival coincided with the barley harvest, and a good crop awaited the reapers. Naomi knew she had made the right decision in returning to Bethlehem; this was where she belonged.

Naomi introduced her daughter-in-law and let it be known how kind Ruth had been to her. The love between them was obvious, and this loyal daughter-in-law soon won the hearts of Naomi's friends. The story soon spread of how Ruth had left her own people and chosen not only to care for Naomi, but to worship the God of Israel. All the while, though, uppermost in Naomi's mind was the question of how two widows would manage on their own. Surely Jehovah would take care of them, but she was still unable to raise herself out of the slough of despondency.

We all go through times when it seems as though everything is going wrong, but God uses those times to shape and mature us. Blessing comes out of suffering and testing. It's immature always to think there's an easy answer or a painless solution to our difficulties. Life will bring setbacks, disappointments and heartaches, but through them our faith is tested and strengthened. We will fail ourselves and others will fail us, but God never fails. Qualities such as patience, endurance and faithfulness are much more valuable than quick solutions and trouble-free living.

A difficult journey

I'll never forget the first overseas journey I made after Arthur died. Kind friends in the United States had invited me back to an annual conference Arthur and I had attended together. I decided to stay two weeks, take my grand-daughter Fiona with me for company, and visit friends and churches in several states. Fiona had made some friends her age on a previous trip and had been corresponding with them ever since, and also had been praying for the money to see them again. Why not present this trip to Fiona as a last, special present to her from Arthur? The timing coincided with Fiona's school break. As I was reading the Bible one day, God gave me a verse that confirmed my decision: 'A good man leaves an inheritance for his children's children' (Prov 13:22).

This was my first time to make the travel arrangements. Arthur had always planned our itinerary, booked our flights, and kept in touch with the various people arranging our engagements. As our departure date drew near, I prayed that God would bring to my mind anything I'd forgotten. Arthur had always carried with him the addresses and telephone numbers of the people with whom we would be staying. I checked our itinerary and found that I didn't have the home phone number of the first family with whom we'd be staying, so I found it and jotted it down.

When we boarded our flight to Washington, DC, Fiona was eager to see her friends and enjoying every minute. I was a bit apprehensive that we were landing in New York en route, which meant going through customs and hauling all our luggage to another plane. My travel agent had assured me, however, that she had arranged for someone to be there to assist us. Besides, my friends were praying for us to have a smooth, trouble-free journey. Father will take care of us, I told myself.

When we walked off the plane at Kennedy International, I looked in vain for our promised assistant. A curt security officer pointed us to a long line in front of customs. As the line crept along, we waited wearily, enduring the cigarette fumes of a passenger behind us who ignored all the no-smoking signs. At last we were cleared, but my heart sank as we approached the baggage claim area. It was in total chaos. Hundreds of people were jostling to find their luggage. It seemed as if the whole world had arrived at one New York airport. Wherever would we find our promised help?

'Come on, Grandma, let's do it ourselves,' Fiona urged. So we clambered over the suitcases strewn around and managed to find our bags and drag them away. I breathed a sigh of relief when we had finally transferred our luggage to the next plane. At last I could relax and anticipate the pleasure of being with friends. Everything was taken care of from here; someone was going to meet us. But relief turned to disappointment when we hurried off the plane to find no one waiting for us.

By this time, my faith was at a low ebb. We were both tired, and I prayed desperately for Father to help us. I needed to telephone our hosts; now I knew why it had been important for me to obtain their phone number. But another obstacle presented itself. In all my previous trips, I had never used an American public phone. Hoping he would not think me stupid, I asked a gentleman using a phone if he would show me what to do. He very kindly went the extra mile and placed the call for me. As it turned out, we had arrived at a different airport than our friends had expected, and someone was waiting for us at the other one!

I decided to take the easy route and hire a taxi for the hour-and-a-half drive to Maryland. Once more, the kind gentleman came to the rescue. He got directions over the phone and wrote them down for the taxi driver. 'I hope you find one who can read,' he said as he carried our suitcases outside. God had the right driver waiting for us, a student who was driving a taxi to earn money in his spare time. Not only was he familiar with the area to which we were going, but he was also quite interested in talking about the Lord. Though I was exhausted, he kept chatting away, asking questions and eager to know more. Fiona, meanwhile, had fallen into a dead sleep. We finally reached our destination at what would have been 2 am our time, fourteen hours after we had left home.

The next morning as I lay in bed, trying to recover from jet lag and my exhaustion from the previous day, I pondered everything that had gone wrong. Why hadn't God answered all those prayers for a smooth journey? Father began to remind me of things I had overlooked. 'You both had wheels on your luggage, so you didn't have to carry them. I provided that kind man to help you. I reminded you to obtain the telephone number. I brought the right taxi driver for you.' In fact, our hosts gave the driver their church's address and the time of the Sunday service. Who knows what eternal value resulted from that divine appointment?

Despite all the unexpected annoyances on our journey, clearly God had been with me at every step. An overwhelming sense of gratitude filled my heart. I later found out that I myself had given my friends the wrong information about our destination. This was for me a lesson in humility and on the need to rely totally on God, not on my confidence in being an experienced traveller! I buried my pride and determined to be more careful in the future. Father understood how hard I found it to do all the things that would have been Arthur's responsibility. If everything had gone right I would not have learned how much he cares. In my head I knew the Lord would always be with me, but as a new widow I was only beginning to experience the security of his love.

God uses every struggle

As we experience the struggles and disappointments that come as we grow older, we need to learn the reason that our expectations are not always fulfilled. God uses every experience to bring us into a deeper relationship with himself. The more we get to know God, the more we can trust that in all things, he works for the good of those who love him (Rom 8:28). When I thought everything was going wrong on my journey, the Lord was there, bringing something good out of it for me. That is a certain promise for all who love him.

Naomi assumed that because everything seemed to go wrong, God was afflicting her. She couldn't understand why. But God is gracious; he never allows us to suffer one moment longer than we are able to bear. Soon Naomi's eyes would be opened, and she would recognise that God had been working on her behalf all along.

Often we can look back on occasions when we suffered loss or disappointment and see the fruit that resulted. Perhaps we gained greater resilience or a deeper confidence in God. So often it's in times of great stress or hardship that we experience God in a deeper way. Only then, it seems, do we really begin to grasp the profound wonder that nothing can separate us from his love. Scripture tells us that suffering tests our faith and produces perseverance, making us mature, complete, not lacking anything (Jas 1:2–4). Sooner or later, a harvest of righteousness and peace will be seen in our lives.

Bible Study: Discovering God's gifts

We take great care in wrapping a gift to send to a friend. The packaging is designed to give rise to the hope that there is something good inside. God's good things are not always like that; they may be cloaked in a package of trials and testings.

Here are some 'wrappings'. Can you suggest the blessing they may contain?

1. Disappointment (see Ps 84:11).
2. Suffering (Rom 5:3–5).
3. Trials (Jas 1:2–4).
4. Insults, persecution, hardship (2 Cor 12:9–10).

We find it hard to thank God for the package. But many of us who have gone through suffering no doubt can testify how through it we discovered the reality of his love in a new way. 1 Peter 1:6–7 sums up the purpose for which our heavenly Father allows us to go through the fire.

5. Discuss any experiences you've had when seeming disappointments proved to be God's means of bringing you into a new experience of his grace.

6. Think of a situation in your life now that you find especially difficult. How do you think God might be using it to your benefit?

11

God at Work for Good

And Ruth the Moabitess said to Naomi, 'Let me go to the fields and pick up the leftover grain behind anyone in whose eyes I find favour.' Naomi said to her, 'Go ahead, my daughter.' So she went out and began to glean in the fields behind the harvesters. As it turned out, she found herself working in a field belonging to Boaz, who was from the clan of Elimelech (Ruth 2:2–3).

Imagine the scene after Naomi and Ruth returned to Bethlehem. Naomi, still in despair, was quite convinced that she had nothing more to offer Ruth. They had found a house and made it as comfortable as possible, given their limited resources. But Naomi's pessimism continued to increase as she saw their food supply dwindle with each passing day. Since she had no ready means of supporting herself and Ruth, their future looked as bleak as it had in Moab. Naomi's spirits sank to their lowest point.

Ruth, meanwhile, tried to encourage Naomi and show her kindness in practical ways. She openly let it be known that her trust was in Jehovah, and her behaviour won the approval of everyone she met.

Volunteering to run errands for her mother-in-law, she soon found her way around the town. Ruth enjoyed settling down in her new environment and took every opportunity to observe people going about their daily business. She observed how the men were reaping in the harvest fields and also noticed young women gleaning behind them.

Perhaps Naomi had taught Ruth about how the law of Moses protected widows; the law encouraged reapers of the harvest not to pick the field clean, but to leave some grain behind for widows, orphans and sojourners (Deut 24:19). Before long Ruth had an idea. She was strong and ready to work as hard as the women she had watched. Why not join them? Eagerly she told Naomi her desire; it was best to make sure she approved.

Imagine Naomi's heart sinking as she listened to Ruth's request, which only served to highlight the helplessness of her widowhood. It would be a humbling step, not to mention a dangerous one, for a young woman to venture out alone among the field hands, but Naomi could think of no alternative. They needed food. She anxiously watched her daughter-in-law set off the next morning. Ruth seemed so confident that Jehovah would take care of her. In her desperation, Naomi prayed for Ruth during what seemed a long day.

Darkest before the dawn

The darkest hour is just before the dawn. Most often when God seems furthest away we are actually very near to finding him. He never allows us to be tested

beyond our strength, but always provides a way out
(1 Cor 10:13). For Naomi, dawn was about to break.

Ruth was tired but brimming with excitement
when she arrived home that evening. She showed
Naomi how much grain she had gathered, and
Naomi could hardly believe her eyes. Naomi prepared their meal while Ruth refreshed herself after
the long, hard day. When they finally sat down
together, Naomi was all ears, and Ruth was eager to
tell her about her day.

Not knowing which field to choose, Ruth prayed
about it, finally deciding on one where the man in
charge looked trustworthy. He readily allowed her
to join the women working there. Following their
example, Ruth soon learned the best method of
gleaning. As the day wore on, the owner of the field
appeared. As she listened to the way he greeted
everyone with 'The Lord be with you' and took a
personal interest in the reapers, Ruth was glad she
had found this field. She felt safe knowing it
belonged to such a godly man. Jehovah had heard
her prayers.

'Then I was taken completely by surprise,' she
told her mother-in-law. 'The owner came over to
speak to me and said he'd heard about me! He told
me to make sure I kept close to his servant girls and
not to go into any other field. He said that whenever
I was thirsty, I could drink from the water jars his
men had filled. His words made me so sure that the
Lord was taking care of me; he told me I had found
a place of refuge under God's wings.'

Naomi was even more astonished to hear how
Ruth was invited to join the owner at mealtime and
partake of his food. She felt so grateful to this man

who had shown her daughter-in-law such kindness. 'What was his name?' she asked. 'Boaz,' Ruth replied, describing her benefactor in detail. It was plain he had made quite an impression on the young woman.

'Boaz!' Naomi exclaimed. 'He's a close relative!' It was almost too much for Naomi to take in. 'The Lord bless him.' Hope rose in Naomi's heart as her eyes were finally opened to the fact that God was with her. He had not stopped caring for her. Suddenly everything had changed. Without any effort on her part, they were now linked with the one man who could help them. Once again, praise rang from Naomi's lips as she expressed her joy and thanksgiving to the Lord.

Naomi was no longer anxious about Ruth's safety because Boaz had invited her to continue gleaning in his field until the harvest was over. As the days went by, Naomi's spirits continued to rise as she observed how happy Ruth was each evening when she came home, and how readily she set out for the fields the next morning.

Perhaps, Naomi thought, there was something she could do for Ruth after all: she could use her position as Boaz's relative to bring him and Ruth together. She wondered if he would be willing to fulfil the role of the 'kinsman-redeemer'. This was the closest male relative of a man who had died, whose duty, by custom, was to take his relative's widow as his wife and raise up children to carry on the dead man's name and inherit his property. Naomi wondered how Ruth would feel about such an arrangement, since Boaz was not a young man.

Emboldened by her restored faith, Naomi felt

convinced the time was right for her to set things in motion. Her womanly insight assured her that despite the differences in age and culture, the relationship between Boaz and Ruth was already blossoming. She wasn't surprised to find her daughter-in-law more than delighted when she offered to seek a home for her with Boaz.

Sometimes we complicate life by relying on our human reasoning. The more we try to work out a solution to a problem, the bigger it becomes. All we can see is the hopelessness of the situation; we are blind to God's presence. Isaiah reminds us that God's thoughts are not our thoughts; they are higher than ours (55:8–9). In other words, human intellect is insufficient. The sooner we fix our thoughts on God himself, the sooner the problem will be solved. A godly man I knew years ago was fond of saying, 'It's easy when God does it.' Naomi was finding that out. The answer wasn't complicated, and it wasn't a plan she engineered herself. God had miraculously brought Boaz into their lives and inclined his heart towards Ruth.

Since the death of her sons, Naomi had wanted to be able to find a husband for Ruth, to see her happily settled in a home of her own. One of the reasons she had tried so hard to dissuade Ruth from coming to Israel was her certainty that, if Ruth stayed with her, the young woman would have no chance to remarry and have a family. Now that very desire was about to be fulfilled.

Until that point, clouds of discouragement had hidden God's love from Naomi's mind. I doubt that she would have been too pleased or very receptive if some well-meaning friend had breezed in to

exhort her that 'all things work together for good'.
But now the sun was breaking through. The hard
things had not disappeared—she was still without
her husband and sons—but now that she felt once
more the warmth of God's love, somehow the bitterness was fading.

Naomi's perspective on her past hadn't instantly
changed. She didn't suddenly see the mourning
and heartache she'd suffered in Moab as a wonderful blessing. The promise in Romans 8:28, that 'in
all things God works for the good of those who love
him' does not mean we should try to convince ourselves by some extraordinary mental gymnastics
that everything bad is really good. We needn't keep
smiling and pretend that what brings despair and
disappointment into our lives has no effect on us.
No one should dismiss the emotional pain that
arises when death or tragedy strikes. But such
things are also the vehicles of God's grace, used by
him to bring us into a deeper experience of his love
and mercy. Naomi did not immediately see how
much God had been with her in her darkest days,
working for her good. That would only come later.

Bible Study: Hope

In English, the words 'I hope so' express uncertainty, a lack of assurance. True biblical hope is just
the opposite: it expresses confidence and expectation. Hope is essential to be able to say, 'We know
God is at work for good in all things.'
1. Here is a prayer and a promise to learn by heart:
'May the God of hope fill you with all joy and peace

as you trust in him, so that you may overflow with hope by the power of the Holy Spirit' (Rom 15:13).

2. What does this verse tell us will be the fruit of hope?

3. Look up Hebrews 6:19, 1 Peter 3:15 and 1 Thessalonians 5:8. How would you explain your hope?

4. How can we strengthen our hope and prepare ourselves for the future? (See 1 Pet 1:13.)

12

God's Abundance

> May the Lord repay you for what you have done. May
> you be richly rewarded by the Lord, the God of Israel,
> under whose wings you have come to take refuge
> (Ruth 2:12).

Little did Naomi realise when she returned to Bethlehem that she was on the brink of a new life of
prosperity, rather than the poverty she assumed
would plague her remaining years. The very circumstances that had restricted and discouraged her
would become the means of bringing her into a
deeper understanding of her Father's steadfast love.

It had all started when Ruth left home, seeking to
glean for leftovers, and instead came back with an
abundance. And that was just the beginning.
Whenever Ruth was in Boaz's field, he instructed
the harvesters to deliberately leave a generous supply of grain for her. Why did Boaz take such pains
to provide for a total stranger? Scripture indicates
he had heard the glowing reports about Ruth—
about the sacrifices she had made, her faith in
Jehovah, her devotion to Naomi. He may also have
been prompted by the knowledge that to help Ruth

would also help his needy relative, Naomi. We can safely assume that the Lord, who has a special desire to care for widows, was at work, drawing Boaz's affection towards Ruth.

A storehouse of good things

As I began to think of how generously God supplied Ruth and Naomi's needs, I was led to Psalm 31:19, which says, 'How great is your goodness, which you have stored up for those who fear you.' God was showing me that he doesn't want us just to scrape by with the meagre necessities. On the contrary, he supplies us out of an abundant store of goodness, which is waiting to meet our needs.

I think it gave God great delight to surprise Naomi with Ruth's sudden good news. It may have reminded her of all the blessings promised to God's people. The Old Testament has many wonderful promises of abundance and security for those who fear the Lord and serve him with wholehearted obedience. Deuteronomy 6:3 says, 'Hear, O Israel, and be careful to obey so that it may go well with you and that you may increase greatly in a land flowing with milk and honey, just as the Lord, the God of your fathers, promised you.' Deuteronomy 26:18–19 admonishes God's people, 'his treasured possession', to keep the Lord's commands and promises that God 'will set you in praise, fame and honour high above all the nations'. Elimelech and Naomi had not disobeyed God's commandments and gone after other gods, as had many Israelites, but Naomi's faith that these promises would be hers had grown dim.

Yet the God who had provided Naomi with a way of escape from Israel's famine was still watching over her. This was the same God who had caused her husband and sons to prosper, then after they died had given her a loving daughter-in-law to care for her, and finally brought them back safely to Bethlehem. And it was this God who had led Ruth to Boaz. Now that the famine was over, Naomi was about to taste of the land's 'milk and honey'. She was enjoying a foretaste of the good things to come, for Boaz was a man of great wealth.

God had an abundance stored up to fill Naomi's needs. He delights to do the same for us, not because we are worthy, but simply because we are in Christ. Our relationship with him is the key to continued fruitfulness in each season of our lives. Jesus tells us, 'Abide in me'—that is, make our relationship with him the focal point of our life— and you will 'bear much fruit' (Jn 15:5). Does this mean that financial success is the barometer of our walk with God? Are we abiding in Christ only when our bank balance is high and nothing goes wrong to threaten our abundance? No, the fruit Jesus is speaking about—the life of Christ manifested in us, whatever our situation—is intended to delight the One who causes this fruit to grow. A grouchy Christian millionaire and a grouchy Christian struggling to pay his bills are equally disappointing to our heavenly Father.

In my teenage years, when I was a new believer, I was fascinated by missionary stories; the amazing accounts of how God supplied their needs in far-off lands were thrilling to me. These men and women told about how they lived by faith, and that created a desire in me to do the same. Like most girls that age, I had some definite ideas about the kind of man I wanted to marry. A handsome husband earning £1,000 a year was every young Englishwoman's dream in those days. High on my list, though, was the desire for someone like my missionary heroes, who felt called to live by faith.

One missionary biography I read gave me the idea of writing down all the qualities I desired in a husband. The book was about John and Betty Stam, two American missionaries martyred in China in the early 1900s. Their courage stirred my imagination and admiration, and Betty's account of how she had listed all the things she wanted in her future partner found an echo in my heart. Arthur fulfilled my request for a man who lived by faith—he was also tall, dark and handsome!

I look back to our early days of married life with gratitude for all the Lord taught me. Learning God's ways gives us a treasury of good things to share. Arthur and I served him full time, ministering in a variety of ways, including writing books, speaking at churches and conferences, helping and encouraging leaders, and sending supplies to missionaries— without any regular means of financial support. Serving the Lord overseas seemed, in my ignorance, more glamorous and exciting, but the thrill of proving God's faithfulness in meeting our needs at home in the UK was just as strengthening to my faith.

Paul's words in Philippians 4:11–13 are instructive:

I have learned to be content whatever the circumstances. I know what it is to be in need, and I know what it is to have plenty. I have learned the secret of being content in any and every situation, whether well fed or hungry, whether living in plenty or in want. I can do everything through him who gives me strength.

In other words, Paul's success was in his relationship with Christ; success was measured by his spiritual contentment, not by material blessing.

The lean years

For tax purposes, Arthur kept careful records of all his income. I came across the oldest records recently, and even allowing for the changing value of the pound, I realised we lived on an incredibly small amount during those first few years. I do remember how often we had little or no money and prayed earnestly that God would meet our needs. We learned to go without amenities, grew our own vegetables, and often wore second-hand clothing. We lived very simply. Our home in a quiet Devon village had no running water, electricity, or gas. After our car was wrecked in an accident, we resorted to bicycles for eight years until a brother in Christ finally bought us another car. Once Arthur didn't have money for a train fare, so he cycled seventy miles to a town where he was scheduled to speak.

Even though we never knew how much would be available from week to week, Arthur and I never felt deprived. The thrill we felt each time God provided for a need never diminished. That's not to say we had no times of difficulty: sometimes God kept us waiting for what seemed to us a tremendously long time, but he was never too late.

I recall one week when I couldn't understand why the Lord hadn't brought in any provision. We had food to eat, but the milkman called for his money every Saturday, and I didn't have enough to pay him. I felt sure a letter with a gift would arrive in the post, but none came. God wanted to teach me he could work in other ways. To my great surprise, that Saturday I found the milk had been left on my doorstep, but no one had knocked to ask for the money. That was the only time I can recall that ever happening! But the next Saturday, God had supplied me with enough to pay for both weeks.

On another occasion, we had made an appointment for our son to see a doctor in a nearby town. Since we were eleven miles away, this entailed a bus trip, but I didn't have enough money for the fare. Arthur was gone, and I knew he would have some money when he returned, but that wouldn't solve the immediate need. Just as I was praying about it, a familiar cry echoed down the street: 'Rags, any old rags?' It was the rag-and-bone man. As quickly as I could, I rummaged in my cupboards for extra linens and old clothing and dashed out just in time to catch him. He gave me the exact amount for our two fares! I'll never forget how thrilled I was.

God sometimes surprised us with a special provision. An earlier chapter mentions how we supplied cassette tapes to people ministering overseas. Most missionaries didn't have high quality tape recorders, so we needed good equipment to produce the tapes. A church in the United States had offered to give us their duplicating equipment at a very low price because they were updating theirs. They sent it to the manufacturer to get it serviced for us, and the manufacturer said he couldn't guarantee the machine would work properly in Britain because of the different electrical voltage. So this church simply sent us a brand new machine, but only charged us the price of a used one. When this state-of-the-art duplicating equipment arrived in our little village, we were the first people in Britain to have anything like it.

As I've already mentioned, as part of this service to missionaries, each year we sent out hundreds of packages filled with food and supplies. We trusted the Lord to supply the money for purchasing and posting these goods. We never appealed for donations; the funds just came in. If we were short of money, we waited to buy the goods until God provided it.

Whether we have a steady income or not, we're all called to live by faith and to recognise that it's God who supplies all our needs. From the start, Arthur and I applied two rules to our finances. First of all, we set aside part of whatever came in as our tithe. That was God's portion, and it was a joy to be able to give to others. Second, we never bought anything unless we actually had the money in hand to pay for it. I believe these two principles taught us wisdom and kept us from running into debt. We reckoned that if Father wanted us to have something, he would send the money. If not, we were content to go without it.

Adjusting to abundance

Television, with its advertisements feeding the desire for all kinds of goodies, had not yet invaded our life, and most shops were miles away. So in our early years, it wasn't difficult to escape the pressure of consumerism. Then life began to change. We began doing better financially; Arthur was in much more demand, and his books were selling well. Adjusting to abundance, though, proved more of a battle for us than coping with little. Christians around us were acquiring modern conveniences, such as washing machines and televisions, and a feeling of superiority began to sour our contentment. Wasn't it more spiritual, we wondered, to go without?

Our vision of God had become warped. Material things in themselves are not evil; it's the love of them that's the problem. It took us a while to realise that our gracious Father delights to give good things to his children. A child clothed in rags demonstrates that his father is unable to provide for him. Having learned to be content, Arthur and I now needed to rejoice in living in the abundance of God's goodness to us. We learned that the same God who met our needs in times of want, often by supplying us with second-hand goods, could actually provide enough for us to buy brand new things. For a time, I even disciplined myself to give up my usual practice of diligently searching all the shops to find the best possible bargain; instead, I made up my mind to pay the full price, accepting and enjoying my Father's generosity, and not to feel obliged to pinch every penny.

One of our biggest tests came when we bought our first house. Having lived for nearly twenty-five years in a somewhat dilapidated rented property, we were thrilled at the prospect of owning a home of our own. Both our parents had died, leaving enough money for us to be able to afford a nice home. The place we found had everything the other lacked. We had longed for sunlight in our rented house, which had little natural light throughout the winter. But sunshine beamed in every room in our new home, and we even had an enclosed sunporch. Our rented land featured only a small vegetable plot. The new property, formerly occupied by an avid gardener, covered more than a third of an acre and featured two beautiful gardens full of flowers, shrubs, vegetables and fruit trees; a goldfish pond with beautiful water lilies; and two greenhouses. What's more, Arthur even had his own study. It seemed like paradise! This was Father's bounty.

Yet Arthur and I found ourselves feeling guilty about living in this pleasant setting. We made excuses, explaining that we had bought the home so missionaries and other guests could enjoy staying there with us. We certainly looked forward to entertaining many guests, but that wasn't the reason God gave us the house. Lovingly, the Lord rebuked us and told us he wanted us to enjoy it for ourselves as his gift. The idea that it was more spiritual to go without had to be cleared from our thinking once and for all. We ended up staying in that home four years. We still went through times when money was limited, but it no longer bothered us if we gave an appearance of prosperity. Like Paul, we were learning to be content in plenty as well as in want.

God makes perfect provision for us; he plans all our days for good. In Christ, we have been granted everything we need for life and godliness (2 Pet 1:3).

For Naomi, the time had come to be released from the burden of want and to enjoy a time of plenty.

Bible Study: Learning to be content

It's easy to maintain a good outlook when things are going well and we feel spiritually on top. But the real condition of our faith is revealed in times of distress and disappointment, or when we face problems that seem insurmountable. Is it possible to be content regardless of our circumstances?

1. Ponder or perhaps memorise Paul's words in Philippians 4:11–12. Write down or discuss what you think his secret was.

2. What was the learning process Paul went through? Make a note of the things mentioned in Philippians 3:7–8 and 4:19.

3. Is it possible for everyone to know God in the same intimate way Paul did? The trials and sufferings he endured taught him about God's ways and character. That is what enabled Paul to trust the Lord in every circumstance. Write down all the aspects of God's character you can think of, such as his kindness and faithfulness. Psalm 145 is a good place to begin your search.

4. If you're in a group, pray for one another and encourage each other to be content in whatever difficulties are facing you now, assured that you are in the hands of the One whose will and ways are in keeping with his character.

5. Read Psalm 37:5 in the Revised Standard Version as well as from another version. Thank the Lord that he moves on behalf of those who put their trust in him. Ask him to help you learn Paul's secret.

13

Put on Your Best Clothes

Wash and perfume yourself, and put on your best
clothes (Ruth 3:3).

Following World War II, it was some years before
Britain's economy got back to normal and shops
were fully stocked again. Most of us became skilled
in the art of 'make do and mend'. Hence I was better
prepared than most young brides would be today to
cope with the very restricted income Arthur and I
had in our early years of marriage. Long after
rationing had ceased, we were still rationed by our
finances. I still remember the thrill when Arthur
was able for the first time to buy me a new dress. I
can picture it even now, a lovely red wool dress.

After surviving so long, though, on a small wardrobe of mostly second-hand clothes, it took some
time to get used to the idea of actually wearing
garments that were new. I would gaze at dresses
hanging in my wardrobe, delighted to know they
were really mine. Occasionally I enjoyed the feel of
their material, but I hardly ever wore them! Instead
of putting on a brand new dress for Sundays, or for
lesser occasions when I needed to dress up, I kept

waiting for that special party or wedding that rarely occurred. I needed to hear my Father say, as did Naomi, 'Put on your best clothes.' That phase of my life finally passed when it dawned on me that I was the daughter of the King and that it gave him pleasure to see me enjoying his provision. My clothes were the outward evidence of a relationship that freed me to receive God's generosity.

A plan

So far, Boaz had only seen Ruth dressed for a hard day's work in the fields. The plan Naomi had in mind called for more than the ancient equivalent of blue jeans, an old shirt and a pair of work gloves. Naomi advised Ruth to wash, make herself look attractive, and pick her most beautiful garments. She was about to initiate a plan for rewarding this young woman who had shown her such loving care and had so faithfully served the Lord. The moment had come to bring Hebraic inheritance law into use. Naomi would give Boaz, her wealthy kinsman, the opportunity to fulfil the role of kinsman-redeemer by buying Elimelech's land and marrying his heir, Ruth.

Dressed in her most beautiful attire, Ruth was to surprise Boaz as he lay sleeping on the threshing floor, telling him of her wish that he fulfil the part of the nearest kinsman. I can imagine Naomi thoroughly enjoying herself as she helped Ruth get ready for this once-in-a-lifetime occasion. Naomi was as excited about this as any of us would be today at the thought of planning a wedding for a loved one. But how would we feel if our first responsibility was to tell the bride-to-be to go and propose to her intended? No doubt many would strongly disapprove of such a brash attempt at matchmaking. Not the done thing in our society!

To understand Naomi's actions, though, we shouldn't view her situation from a twentieth-century perspective. She lived several thousand years ago in a culture in which matchmaking was the rule. Though sending Ruth to visit Boaz might seem odd or bewildering to believers today, rest assured Naomi was not being an interfering mother-in-law, but was acting within the guidelines of the law. Because of the cultural gap, it's not completely clear why Ruth went at night to meet Boaz in secret. But we can trust that Naomi's motives were pure and that she was confident that Ruth and Boaz could both be trusted to behave honourably, which they did.

What to wear?

Often a woman's first thought when she's invited to some important function is 'What shall I wear?' There's nothing wrong with the desire to be appropriately dressed. We are free to wear something we will enjoy. It is only when concern about our appearance dominates our thinking, coming to matter more than pleasing God, that it becomes a hindrance to our relationship with him. Jesus said, 'Why do you worry about clothes? See how the lilies of the field grow. They do not labour or spin. Yet I tell you that not even Solomon in all his splendour was dressed like one of these' (Mt 6:28–29). We're not to fret about our clothes, but to trust our heavenly Father to provide what we need. God's choice will be as attractive as the lilies of the field.

God taught me the reality of that passage in Matthew when I was engaged, shortly after World War II. Clothes rationing was still enforced, and I didn't have enough coupons to buy a wedding dress and clothes for our honeymoon, so I prayed about the matter rather anxiously. I decided what kind of dress I wanted the moment Arthur showed me a wedding photo of a friend of his who had recently married. The bride's dress was my idea of the perfect gown, and I longed for something like it. Imagine my joy a few weeks later when I learned this bride wanted to sell her dress. Worn just once, it was as good as new, and no coupons were required. My heavenly Father had heard my prayer.

The next surprise came when some of Arthur's mother's friends in the United States wrote a letter asking for my measurements. A package from them arrived during my last term at Bible college, and my fellow students crowded around to watch me open it. There were 'ooh's' and 'aah's' as I unwrapped a dress and some elegant lingerie. Then, we all gasped in awe as I took out a long, flowing silk negligée. I haven't had one as beautiful since! With these items taken care of, I had more than enough coupons to buy the rest of my honeymoon clothes.

Inward and outward beauty

To most women, dress will always be important. Clothing oneself is a natural outlet for our creativity and love of beauty and is one of the ways in which we can help make our message, the gospel, attractive. Without the inner beauty of a meek, gentle and quiet spirit, though, there's always the risk of attracting undue attention to our appearance. But being careless about how we look also carries the same risk. Some Christians feel strongly that being overly concerned about clothing is pandering to the flesh. We have latitude for different opinions, so let each woman be fully persuaded in her own mind and not make something unessential into a major issue.

What guidelines are given for those who want to please the Lord in all things, set the right example, and be worth following in our manner of dress? Naomi's instructions to Ruth encouraged her to enjoy being a woman, to forget her work clothes and put on something feminine. Ruth had no trouble following her advice, but I do know of women who find it hard to dress in a style that expresses their femininity. For various reasons, they resent being women, hate themselves, and express their rejection by the way they dress. Through understanding and wise counsel, along with practical assistance, such women can be released into a new liberty and experience of self-worth. Spiritual growth and healing is bound to affect a person's outward appearance. Let's be ready to help each other enjoy our femininity.

The rule of grace

In the matter of clothing, as with everything else, we are not under law but under grace. Grace enables us to offer every part of our bodies to God as instruments of righteousness. There is no set of rules to obey, but a new master to serve, one whom we love to please. Paul tells us in Romans 7:6 that we have been released from the law: we now serve in the new way of the Spirit, not in the old way of the written code.

Scripture tells us to seek such clothing as is fitting for the bride of Christ. Revelation 19:7–8 says, 'The wedding of the Lamb has come, and his bride has made herself ready. Fine linen, bright and clean, was given her to wear.' (Fine linen stands for the righteous acts of the saints.) Other scriptures say we are wrapped in a robe of righteousness and a mantle of praise, clothed with the humility of Christ and in garments of power and salvation (Is 61:3,10; Lk 24:49; 1 Pet 5:5).

Ruth obeyed Naomi's instructions to the letter, a sign of the confidence she placed in the older woman. Naomi was a wise woman. People do observe the way others dress; in fact, it's one of the first things people notice when they meet someone new. Ruth had never had any cause to doubt Naomi's judgement; Naomi's whole lifestyle was attractive and consistent with the faith she professed. So when the issue of what to wear came up, she could follow her advice without hesitation.

Another exemplary woman

The woman of noble character we read about in Proverbs 31 offers us another example to follow. First we learn that she made sure her family was adequately supplied with warm clothing for the winter. Such a woman wouldn't be caught by surprise by the first snowstorm; no frantic dash to the shops for a new pair of boots for Tommy, no sinking feeling from finding that little Beth's winter coat is much too small. This woman had no fear because she was prepared, and that added to the security of her household. God sometimes supplies our needs in an emergency by enabling us to plan wisely beforehand. Philippians 4:6 reminds us of this: 'Pray about everything, tell God your needs, and don't forget to thank him for the answers' (TLB).

The next thing we learn about this woman of excellence is that her clothing was made of fine linen and purple, materials fit for a queen. They were high quality garments. Her clothing wasn't the result of a self-indulgent spending spree, but was her reward for cultivating the skill of her own hands. Our lesson here is that a few basic items of the best quality we can afford provide a good framework on which to build a practical wardrobe.

Finally, this woman is described as 'clothed with strength and dignity'. Trusting the Lord, she was free from apprehension about the future and full of joyous expectation. Those who met her found their faith stirred by her confidence in God and the wholesome atmosphere she created. She was worthy of honour and respect.

Beautiful clothing cannot produce character, but what we wear sometimes speaks volumes. Matthew 6:28–29 reminds us that God has clothed the lilies of the field in even greater splendour than Solomon in all his glory. There's nothing I enjoy more as a hobby than to see the beauty of creation, to walk where wild flowers abound, observe the birds in their spring colours, watch with awe one of the marvellous nature programmes showing the paradise of colours hidden under the ocean. Yet we are more precious to our heavenly Father than any of these. Taking too much trouble over what to wear can be sheer vanity. On the other hand, not to bother at all could mean we neither value ourselves nor appreciate that God takes delight in us (Ps 147:11).

Bible Study: A matter of choice

Nationality, occupation and financial status, age and sex, religion, character—these are among the things revealed by the clothes we wear. It's important that your appearance be in keeping with the faith you profess.

1. Look up these scriptures: 1 Peter 3:3 and 5:5, Isaiah 61:3,10, Luke 24:49, Psalm 45:9,13–14 and 1 Timothy 2:9. Note that they connect the inner self with the outward appearance.

2. We know that it is more important to be concerned with inward beauty, so make a list of the inner 'garments' you would like to have in your wardrobe.

3. Discuss or write down what practical advice you would give to a young woman who wanted help in choosing the right clothes to buy.

4. Enjoy sharing the lessons you have learned and mistakes you have made with your wardrobe. Make any comments that might be helpful in the light of the above scriptures and others you may find applicable.

5. Pray for one another that in your outward appearance you may shine as lights in the world and glorify our Saviour.

14

What Am I Worth?

All my fellow townsmen know that you are a woman
of noble character (Ruth 3:11).

Ruth must have been apprehensive as she set off for
the threshing floor where Boaz and his men were
winnowing the barley. Remembering Naomi's
instructions, she kept out of sight in the shadows,
watching to see where Boaz would rest. Not until all
the men were sleeping soundly did she pluck up the
courage to go and lie at his feet. What would he say
when he discovered her and heard her request?
After all, she was merely a foreigner, one of many
women who gleaned in his fields. Her mind told her
it was foolish to think he would desire her in marriage, but somehow her confidence was growing
now that she had stepped out in faith. Would
Jehovah care enough to incline Boaz's heart towards
her? She would find out soon. There was no turning
back.

Ruth slipped on to the threshing floor and found
her way to Boaz. Suddenly he stirred, awakened by
her presence. 'Who are you?' he asked. Trembling,
she gave her name and told him why she had come.

Her fear turned to joy as Boaz asked Jehovah to bless her and urged her not to be afraid. He was more than willing to comply with her request. There was just one obstacle: Boaz would first have to find out if another man, one who was a closer kinsman, wished to marry her.

Ruth, assured by Boaz's promise to speak to the man in the morning, settled back to sleep. Just before daylight, she arose to go home, making sure she wasn't seen. 'You can't go back home without taking a present for Naomi,' Boaz told her as he filled her shawl with a generous gift of barley. The bundle was heavy, but the joy in her heart made the burden seem light.

All the way home she reflected on the thrill of that night. Her delight wasn't only in that Boaz had agreed to marry her, but in the reason he had given for his readiness to do so. 'All the people know you as a woman of noble character,' he had said. His words left no doubt that such was his opinion as well. This compliment, coming from such a godly man, overwhelmed her. She treasured it in her heart as she hurried home to tell Naomi the wonderful news.

Waiting it out

Naomi and Ruth rejoiced together at this marvellous turn of events; then their thoughts turned to the question of whether Elimelech's other relative, not Boaz, would serve as kinsman-redeemer. How Ruth longed to know who her future husband would be. Even though Boaz was an older man, the thought of being his wife filled her with happiness and peace. If only she could do something to ensure that the other man bowed out! Naomi did her best to comfort Ruth, but the matter was no longer in their hands. 'Just wait as patiently as you can,' Naomi advised Ruth. 'There's no need to fret. Boaz will want to settle this today.'

Most of us are not naturally endowed with an ample supply of patience, yet faith and patience go hand in hand. We learn how much we need patience when our faith is tested in situations that require us to persevere. James tells us that through perseverance we become mature (Jas 1:4).

As we get older, the difficulties that come our way provide opportunities for building our patience and endurance; our faith is stretched and strengthened. The steadying influence of a mature Christian helps curb the kind of youthful enthusiasm that is over-anxious to get on with things. Experience had taught Naomi to wait for God's moment and to look to him to act. Now she was able to influence Ruth to follow her example.

Boaz's generous gift, sent especially to Naomi, was his recognition of the important part she was playing. The compliment he paid Ruth was the fruit of her mother-in-law's influence. Ruth's desire to follow Naomi had brought out the best in her character. Naomi wasn't too old or useless; far from it. Boaz's gift was tangible evidence that God still intended to use her.

Why notice me?

Like many women, Ruth may have undervalued herself. 'Why should you take any notice of me?'

she had asked Boaz when they first met. As a foreigner, she assumed she would be treated as inferior—tolerated perhaps, but kept outside the privileged circle of naturally born Israelites.

Imagine Ruth's thoughts as she compared herself to the women she saw every day. 'I'm not one of them. I don't even look like them. I'm just a poor widow without even any children.' But to her surprise, she learned that her value to the people of Bethlehem had nothing to do with status, or nationality. She discovered that the things that made her different had drawn not only people's attention but also their commendation. The way she conducted herself in spite of her difficult circumstances revealed her noble character. Take note: neither Ruth's talents nor her achievements won her praise, but her character. Be encouraged. Your true worth isn't revealed by your position, title, wealth, talents, or looks; it's reflected in your manner of living.

What's it worth?

The Antiques Roadshow assembles a group of experts who travel around Britain talking to ordinary citizens about their antiques. Everyone on the programme of course wants to know the answer to that enduring question, 'What's it worth?' Only a trained expert can accurately estimate the value of that colourful vase inherited from Aunt Nellie or the strange silver gadget Grandpa kept locked in his cabinet for sixty years. Value depends on many different factors—age, workmanship, materials, and the reputation of the craftsman. Each item has to be appraised by the proper expert.

Just as a glassware connoisseur may have little inkling of the enormous value of a rare coin, we have little idea of our value as women. God values us by very different standards than does someone who uses only the world's standards. Only our Creator understands the supreme value he places on each person he has made. So don't be swayed by any thoughts or opinions that diminish your self-worth. Accept the judgement of the chief expert: you're priceless!

Arthur and I discovered in our travels that things thrown into the rubbish in one household can be greatly prized in another. Once when we were on holiday in the Ozark Mountains of Arkansas, a friendly American invited us inside to see the house he had built. As he proudly showed us the finishing touches he was adding, my eye caught sight of a vaguely familiar object fixed to the kitchen ceiling. A closer look revealed it to be an enamel colander serving as a lampshade. As we looked around, we saw other 'treasures' on display, everything from old brass door locks to long-outdated telephone equipment. What was of absolutely no value to me was precious to this man. Likewise, though we might see little value in ourselves, God deems us his precious possessions.

I once read about a young couple who bought a house, and, in the process of clearing out the rubbish left in the attic, discarded a pile of rough pencil sketches. They later learned that the artist had become famous. What they thought was worthless was valued at thousands of dollars! We can easily make the mistake of undervaluing ourselves. What the world might put on the scrapheap, God has chosen to accomplish his mighty purposes. No one, however weak or foolish, is insignificant in God's estimation.

Churches frequently ask me to speak about the value and role of women. So often I find that women feel worthless unless they have a label—Sunday school teacher, administrator, secretary, speaker, choir leader or whatever—as if what we do is proof of our value. When something happens to prevent us from continuing in that position, we flounder and long once again to have a 'role' we can label. I felt completely lost for months after Arthur died, not knowing what my role was without him. It took me a while to realise I didn't have to change. I didn't have to acquire a new label. I could simply be myself, a mother, and let my role as an older woman emerge naturally. That's what Naomi did; her only role was to enjoy being a mother to Ruth.

The difficulties Christian women have in this respect arise from the pressure we feel today from a world that despises the feminine role. We're urged to be someone, to do something, anything but be 'just a woman'. The implication that womanhood is not worthwhile is subtle and hard to combat without confidence in our value as Christian women.

God's judgement of us: 'very good!'

The Bible's opening chapter tells us that God created man and woman in his image (Gen 1:26). This is a privilege not given to any other created being.

Women, no less than men, bear the image of God

himself. The Creator looked with pleasure at both Adam and Eve and pronounced them 'very good'. But due to the consequences of Eve's sins, women have for centuries suffered the loss of self-worth. Only in Christ can women be fully restored and enjoy their true equality. Eve's role was that of 'helper'; she was subordinate to a man, but in no way inferior. We must not confuse subordination with inferiority. Scripture teaches all of us to submit to Christ as Head and at times to one another. Somehow a label has been attached saying 'for women only'! However much our heads acknowledge that we are all equal in Christ, to be subordinate conjures up for some women the fear of restriction and inability to find their full potential. In fact true submission will free us to function with greater liberty. The reason is simple—God does not call us to live or serve in isolation, but in relationship.

Peter expresses it beautifully in his first epistle: 'Live in harmony with one another' (3:8). Perfect harmony results when each member of an orchestra follows the conductor and blends in with the rest. Paul uses the illustrations of a body, a spiritual house and an army, to enable us to understand how God plans to use us in harmony together. My heavenly Father made me as I am and has a place that is tailor-made for me, just as he wanted it to be (1 Cor 12:18). I am not inferior or superior, just essential! When I joyfully accept my place as a woman, chosen for a purpose, my potential becomes as great as his purpose for the whole body. I could not accomplish that on my own.

We need to keep our eyes on our Captain Jesus

and let go of these fears. They are like weights that prevent a runner participating at her best. And don't forget, every man has to do the same!

Satan is still directing most of his effort towards woman, for she represents his downfall. His influence lies behind every effort to degrade and despise womanhood. The very creature who gave Satan his opportunity to spoil God's handiwork has become the instrument which heralds his destruction; for Christ, who was born of Mary, came to 'crush his head' (Gen 3:15). While we should not worship Mary, we should recognise how she demonstrates our worth as women. No man could have been chosen as the vessel for bringing the Saviour into the world. How stupid to value ourselves only if we can emulate men or compete on identical terms!

The owner of a priceless treasure places it in the safekeeping of someone trustworthy. But God places his 'treasure' within men and women—fragile, unworthy, and aptly described as 'jars of clay' (2 Cor 4:7). Then he puts them on display before all the world, and through them his power and glory are demonstrated!

Let's get the proper perspective and cease to be influenced by the distorted vision of a world still dominated by the Evil One. A person's worth has nothing to do with sex, ability, position or anything this world commends. It has all to do with our relationship with Christ.

Paul declares everything to be rubbish compared with the surpassing greatness of knowing Christ (Phil 3:8), in whom are hidden all the treasures of wisdom and knowledge (Col 2:3). As his chosen women, we have access to this treasure of power,

wisdom and knowledge. We will rob ourselves of
this treasure if we think it is only for leaders' wives
or exceptionally gifted people. It's not what we do
but the manner in which we live that earns for us a
value worth 'far more than rubies' (Prov 31:10). Our
worth is not to be estimated in human terms, but
only by him who values us so highly that he paid
for our lives with the death of his beloved Son, our
Kinsman-Redeemer.

Bible Study: A valuable helper

'It is not good for the man to be alone. I will make a
helper suitable for him' (Gen 2:18). Many who read
these words assume that God intends an inferior
role for every woman because she is destined to be
'only a helper'. As a result, some very capable
women have felt frustrated and limited in their service to Christ. Let's dispel this misconception by
taking a closer look at what Scripture says about
helpers.

Sooner or later each of us will be in need of help
of some kind. No one is born with the ability to do
everything alone. There are two kinds of help. First,
a helping hand. This is someone who assists you in
a task. You know what to do, but you cannot manage alone. Such help is of great value. Second,
expert assistance. This is given by those who know
more about a task than you do and can perhaps
teach you how to do it. Their knowledge and
experience is invaluable.

I doubt that any of us would describe either of
these 'helpers' as inferior, nor may we conclude that
women fall only in the first category.

1. Who is the 'perfect helper' referred to more often in Scripture than anyone else? (See Ps 33:20, 46:1 and 121:1,2.)

2. What does 1 Corinthians 12:28 teach us?

3. Why did Paul highly commend Phoebe? (See Rom 16:1–2.) What qualities make a good helper?

4. Discuss the following verses and any others on this topic you can find: Ecclesiastes 4:9–10, Isaiah 41:13, Acts 18:27–28, 2 Corinthians 1:10–11 and Hebrews 4:16 and 13:6. There are many more scriptures on this subject, so it is worth doing some additional research if you have the opportunity.

15

Wedding Bells and Lasting Joy

So Boaz took Ruth and she became his wife. And the Lord enabled her to conceive and she gave birth to a son. The women said to Naomi: 'Praise be to the Lord, who this day has not left you without a kinsman-redeemer. May he become famous throughout Israel! (Ruth 4:13–14).

After Ruth had gone home, Boaz hastened to the city gate, a place where respected men gathered to discuss the affairs of the day and conduct important business. Boaz, a man of integrity, wanted everything done openly, so he made sure the townspeople were there to witness what took place. Boaz met with Elimelech's other relative and laid the facts before him. Was he willing to redeem the land that had belonged to Elimelech? At first he agreed to do so. But once he learned that he would be required to marry the widow of Elimelech's son, he backed out, realising that any child he and Ruth might have would become an heir to his property. This would reduce the inheritance for children he already had. His refusal cleared the way for Boaz to marry Ruth.

To legalise the agreement, the men performed an

ancient Hebrew custom. Elimelech's relative removed his sandal and passed it to Boaz. The people rejoiced, declaring that they were witnesses to this important event, and prayed that God would bless the marriage of Boaz and Ruth. With local customs satisfied, everyone was assured that the wedding would be proper. The fanfare at the city gate made this surprise wedding announcement quite a memorable event—as is the case also in traditional weddings today, where family and friends serve as witnesses to this important milestone and pray for God's blessing and seal of approval.

Help needed

Planning a wedding these days involves hard work and careful preparation, usually beginning months in advance. Usually a bride-to-be can find someone older to whom she can turn for advice. I know of several churches where experienced 'wedding advisers' have been appointed to ensure that nothing is overlooked and everything runs smoothly on the great day. There's much delight in attending a wedding where Jesus is the most welcome guest and his presence pervades the atmosphere.

Sadly, many couples today have chosen to do away with the idea of marriage in order simply to live together. It seems an easy option: no fuss or headaches. No expensive receptions. People can just leave whenever they tire of the situation or when conflict arises. Why go to all the trouble and expense of a wedding when all that's required is a genuine love for one's partner? Such reasoning stems from not understanding the true requirement of genuine love, namely a willingness to sacrifice self-interest and to be faithful for a lifetime. The fruit of an uncommitted relationship is lasting insecurity.

In the past decade, moral values have slipped like a landslide, and society suffers the inevitable consequences: rising divorce rates, emotionally wounded children, juvenile delinquency, drug abuse. These problems can be traced in large part to failure to adhere to God's laws for marriage.

From poverty to prominence

When Ruth heard the news that she was to be wed, it must have seemed like a wonderful dream come true. A poor widow from a foreign country, she was to become the wife of one of Bethlehem's most wealthy and respected citizens. She must have been the envy of the town's eligible ladies. But there was no question that Ruth deserved a reward for the way she had cared for her mother-in-law, the woman who had made all this possible.

But what about Naomi? She was selling her most important possession, her land. Naomi could have held on to her field and used it to support herself in her later years. It was both a risk and a sacrifice to give up her own inheritance for Ruth's sake. But she chose to pass it on to Ruth and, in so doing, open a way for future generations to benefit from the land. Naomi chose to deny herself and risk losing her means of livelihood, but she won a blessing far greater than anything she could have gained for herself. Not only did Boaz and Ruth provide for her, but she found a new role that renewed her vitality and filled her with great joy in her old age. Naomi was no longer the despondent woman who felt she had no family, no future, and nothing to offer people, for she was soon to become a grandmother.

When that wonderful day arrived, the women of Bethlehem gathered around as Naomi cradled her precious grandson in her arms. Not only did they give thanks to the Lord for this child, but they prayed a prophetic prayer for him. Little did they know the import of their words, 'May he become famous throughout Israel!' Then they added their own assessment of Ruth's worth. Noting how much Ruth loved Naomi, they declared she was worth more than seven sons. That was quite a commendation, especially at a time when women were greatly undervalued.

That little baby cradled in Naomi's arms was destined to be the grandfather of King David, from whose lineage came the Messiah, the Kinsman-Redeemer foreshadowed by Boaz. Without knowing it, Naomi's sacrifice demonstrated the principle of the cross. Her deed anticipated Jesus' words, 'If anyone would come after me, he must deny himself and take up his cross daily and follow me. For whoever wants to save his life will lose it, but whoever loses his life for me will save it' (Lk 9:23–24).

Learning to let go

As we enter our middle and later years, we often face the danger of clinging too long to positions or responsibilities that have been fruitful for us. Learning graciously to let something go is often much harder than beginning something new. We may have always done something with excellence, but that's no reason to assume it will be our job for the rest of our life. The time comes when we must prune our activities to give our best to the one task that is most significant.

Perhaps you've always handled Christmas dinner; your secret recipe for mincemeat is superb; and as for the Christmas pudding, who else could produce such a delectable product? So every year, you stick to the same menu. After all, Christmas wouldn't be the same if you didn't. Or would it? Maybe the time has come for you to be willing to be entertained. Maybe it's time to get out of a rut and fit in for a change with a younger generation's idea of the ideal menu.

The lesson also applies in the church. How would I feel if my pastor suggested that I turn over to someone younger the Bible study group I've been leading for so many years? Am I ready to invest my talents in helping someone else develop as a leader? Am I ready to rejoice if she makes rapid progress and receives more praise than I did? It's hard to let go, but when we do, we reap a much greater harvest. That Bible study we lead may be the kernel of wheat that has to fall to the ground and die in order to produce many seeds (Jn 12:24).

When we operated Supply Line, the missionary supply service based in our home, I prided myself in the way I organised the work. I had developed the system into a fine art, especially packing the food for shipment. I had taught a group of helpers how to make maximum use of the space in each box. But the time came when I needed to relinquish this ministry to others.

A couple with foreign mission experience took over and ran Supply Line full time, continuing to use our former home as a base of operation. To my great joy, they not only kept things going, but also improved and expanded the ministry. To begin with, they made adjustments reflecting the emphasis in our circle on the importance of the local church. This caused the operation's focus to shift from the individual needs of missionaries to serving the local churches they sought to establish.

Supply Line then began sending leaders to help plant and strengthen churches in places like India and Africa, and also brought pastors from other nations to England for a period of training. They began as well to send out construction teams to help build churches, orphanages and other church facilities.

After many years of experience, I had become an expert at managing the Supply Line operation. It's easy to start thinking that nobody else can organise something as well as we can, but new people and new ideas bring improvements. Now an even better system has been developed in which local churches send supplies to missionaries with whom they have relationships. Supply Line's operation has been adjusted to serve the church better. The couple who took it over and others who followed them would have been hampered in making these significant improvements if I had not been given the grace to let go of the reins.

Whatever our particular ability, it will die with

us if we fail to pass our secrets on to those who come after us. What greater thrill could there be than to see some young woman we have influenced growing in stature and godliness and taking a major part in God's plan for his church? Such fruit will last long after we have gone to be with Christ. This lesson is one even the youngest of us needs to learn.

Investing in children

Old age need not be something we dread, for it brings golden opportunities to play our part in bringing the kingdom of God to earth by investing in the next generation. The Bible records that Timothy's faith was first learned from his grandmother (2 Tim 1:5). Naomi's later years were spent caring for her grandson and teaching him, just as she had taught her own sons and daughter-in-law. Ruth had watched Naomi's life and decided to follow her, and had no qualms about the kind of influence she would have on Obed. Not all of us have been blessed with grandchildren, but we can all take an interest in the children around us. They need the encouragement and godly example an older person can provide.

Arthur was seldom ill, but he was in bed with an infection and feeling very lethargic one day when our grand-daughter Katrina, who was then about four years old, came to spend the night. As soon as she was awake the next morning, she burst into our bedroom full of life, determined to make Grandpa better. She chattered away and sang him her favourite songs. It was just the tonic Arthur needed, and he soon regained his energy.

Some women have expressed to me their dread at being called 'Grandma'. I don't understand their objection, unless they somehow get the notion that they suddenly age the moment a grandchild is born. I've found that just the opposite is true. Just as my husband was revived by Katrina's buoyant enthusiasm for life, I've found that our two grand-daughters have kept me on my toes.

Once on a trip to northern England we stopped for lunch at my son's home. I had taken my turn at the wheel, and because we weren't stopping long I hurried into the house still wearing the comfortable old shoes I kept especially for driving. The two little girls flung their arms around us in their usual exuberant welcome. Then gazing down at my feet with disapproval written all over her face, Katrina, who was about seven at the time, said, 'Grandma, are those the only shoes you've got?'

Wearing the right clothes may be a minor way of influencing our grandchildren, but such comments serve to remind us of how observant they are. Angry words, critical comments, insincerity, and failure to keep promises do not commend our faith to these little ones. We need to be the kind of women our grandchildren will find worth following.

God gave the Israelites instructions to keep his commandments in their hearts and talk about them wherever they went, so that each generation would learn from their parents (Deut 6:6–9). That's good advice for us, too. Let us 'tell the next generation the praiseworthy deeds of the Lord, his power, and the wonders he has done' (Ps 78:4). Children love a good story and will enjoy every detail of true life experience even more. We have a priceless opportunity and responsibility to impart faith to them. In the New Testament, Timothy's mother and grandmother are both mentioned briefly for their influence on Timothy's life (2 Tim 1:5).

Naomi's friends offered her a blessing when her grandson was born: 'May he renew your life and sustain you in old age.' We do receive fresh joy as we invest in the next generation.

There is a work to be done right to the end of our days. As a mother, grandmother, or Sunday school worker, you may be influencing a child chosen to play a special part in fulfilling God's purposes. Children are highly valued in God's kingdom. Jesus rebuked his disciples when they wanted to send the children away; he made it abundantly clear that children are very important to him.

Let us firmly resist the modern voices that call women to rise up and throw off the shackles of motherhood, as if those who choose to stay at home were adopting an inferior lifestyle. There are no superior or inferior roles for women. God desires to use each one of us, whatever our status, to demonstrate to a dying world what it means to be alive, vibrant and fulfilled.

Bible Study: Who's the greatest?

Royalty, heads of state and celebrities regularly receive special attention and honour. Few of us are likely to be regarded as great in the secular world, so we miss such recognition. But I think most of us would happily choose the VIP treatment from friends and loved ones on special occasions, rather than constantly to be in the public eye.

1. Galatians 3:28 says we are all one in Christ, so are there really any VIPs in God's kingdom? When Jesus discovered his disciples arguing about this very subject, he gave them a lesson on true greatness. Read these verses and find out who the special people are: Matthew 18:1–6; Mark 9:33–37.

2. Discuss the above verses. What do we need to learn from Jesus' teachings?

3. Children are impressionable. Matthew 18:5–6 reminds us that it is an awesome responsibility to be entrusted with their care. Discuss the most important ways in which you influence children (see 2 Tim 1:5 and Tit 2:3–4).

4. Many mothers face the difficult question of whether to go to work and leave their children with a child-minder. In the light of what we have been studying, what do you think are the most important factors to consider before making such a choice?

It isn't only mothers, grandmothers and church workers who have the opportunity to influence children. Have you the names of any children on your prayer list? If not, ask God to show you which ones you can pray for and seek to influence. Think of some practical ways of doing this, such as remembering birthdays, finding out particular children's hobbies, and taking an interest in them.

5. The words we speak often leave an indelible impression on the children who listen. Discuss how we can have a good influence through our speech. Consider the following verses: Ephesians 4:25,29, James 1:19 and 3:10, and Deuteronomy 6:4–7.

6. Discuss some practical examples of the need to guard your words. Read and discuss any other scriptures you have found helpful.

16

Serving the Purpose of God

> But one thing I do: Forgetting what is behind and straining towards what is ahead, I press on towards the goal to win the prize for which God has called me heavenwards in Christ Jesus (Phil 3:13–14).

Another year has begun, and I am still trying to finish this book. There have been times when I have thoroughly enjoyed writing and other times when I felt like giving up. My excuses for laying the writing aside for a while could have been quite plausible, because I could easily have filled my time with other important tasks. The one thing that has enabled me to persevere has been the certainty in my own mind that God was telling me to finish this before beginning other projects. I am not a naturally disciplined person and have often fallen into the trap of starting a number of things without completing the first one. I knew instinctively I should not digress this time. How grateful I am to be free to limit myself to one priority.

We all go through phases when we have to keep several plates spinning: cooking dinner, answering the phone, holding a crying baby, supervising the

repairman, helping the children with their home-
work and sorting the washing—all at the same
time! Days like that are sometimes unavoidable. But
we do need to beware of becoming over-committed.
Am I agreeing to add another task to an already
demanding schedule just to satisfy an insatiable
desire to keep busy? Or, when a friend rushes in
with a breathless request for help, then dashes out
to complete her next pressing task, do I feel guilty
because I actually had some spare time to help her?
How many of us dare answer 'no' to the question,
'Have you had a busy day?' 'Busy' has come to be
synonymous with serving the Lord and being
fulfilled and fruitful. One of my difficulties in stick-
ing to writing had been the desire to be a little more
'busy'. God doesn't necessarily want us to be busy;
he wants us to fulfil the role of his choosing.

The older we get, the less 'plate spinning' we
attempt. Our physical limitations force us to
acknowledge that we can't do as much as we once
did. But the limited number of projects we take on
will often be more fruitful and satisfying than our
hectic 'plate spinning' of previous years. God
desires to prune from our lives things that are not
fruitful. Jesus put it this way: 'I am the true vine and
my Father is the gardener. He cuts off every branch
in me that bears no fruit, while every branch that
does bear fruit he trims so clean that it will be even
more fruitful' (Jn 15:1–2). That's a lovely picture of
what can happen to us in our mature years if we are
prepared to let God do the necessary pruning. And
we don't have to wait to be physically unable to
cope before appreciating the wisdom of pruning.

It took me several years to learn to tackle only the

tasks I could accomplish well rather than doing several hastily completed jobs that often required additional work later on. Arthur, on the other hand, was good at giving himself to a task completely until it was finished. He was never satisfied with an imperfect product. But he also made the mistake of thinking he could put a quart into a pint pot, so he seldom finished what he was doing in the time he had estimated. We both learned lessons from our weaknesses that we shared with other 'busy' servants of the Lord.

One of the solutions Arthur and I found was occasionally to set aside time to wait on God together, pray about our commitments, and quietly listen to what God was saying. We would write down everything that occupied our time, then prayerfully go through the list. Some priorities always remained on the list, such as time for family relationships. But most could be laid aside if the time had come to let them go. One by one we went through the items and crossed out whatever God showed us was not essential. Then we made a list of the things God gave us peace about continuing and adding anything fresh he had shown us. Last of all, we asked him to help us establish his priorities.

Each time we did this, the list usually became shorter. We learned that being more fruitful does not mean doing more things, but doing the things God has chosen in a more effective way. That's why the heavenly Gardener loves pruning. He is after luscious, mature fruit, not a lot of little sour grapes that never fully ripen.

It takes time for fruit to mature. If we pick it too soon in our impatience to enjoy the taste, we are only disappointed. Our heavenly Gardener is never impatient but waits for that 'ripe' moment. He allows us to go through periods when we feel laid aside and ignored. In our desire to be fruitful, it is easy to rush in too soon, seize a chance to do something for the Lord—only to find the 'taste' is disappointing. It was not the 'ripe' moment. Better to be still, wait, ready to go forth when he sends us. Then our fruit will be mature, its taste sweet to our soul and a delight to his heart.

A last glimpse

The last glimpse the Bible gives of Naomi finds her in a restful pose. It's a picture that could be found in almost any family photo album: a happy grandmother holding her little grandson. The caption might read 'Grandma enjoying retirement'. No longer busy 'spinning plates', Naomi was able to give herself to just one person: little Obed. In this stage of life, Naomi appeared to be taking life easy, doing as she pleased and perhaps graciously offering a helping hand or a word of counsel when needed. That's an idyllic and perhaps somewhat unrealistic picture of being a grandmother. Nevertheless, it does contain an element of truth: enjoying our 'unbusy' lives can be one of our most valuable contributions. Sitting contentedly with Obed in her arms, Naomi had been entrusted with her last and most fruitful task: influencing the generations to come. I recall once reading a child's definition of a grandparent: 'someone who has time to sit and listen and do things with me'. Most of us are still leading fairly full lives when the first grandchildren arrive. It isn't a wearisome task, but a great joy to be available to 'sit and listen and do things' with our grandchildren. Put it on your priority list or some day you'll regret that you missed the opportunity.

God's purpose

Arthur loved to quote these words: 'If you would make the greatest success of your life, try to discover what God is doing in your time, and fling yourself into the accomplishment of his purpose and will.' Acts 13:36 records that David served the purpose of God in his generation and then died, his task accomplished. God's purpose is centred in Christ, through whom and in whom he will 'bring all things in heaven and on earth together under one head' (Eph 1:10). Christ is the Head of the church, his body on earth, and the church is the means whereby God will accomplish his plan to rule the world in righteousness. Naomi was one of many playing a part in that plan, though without knowing it, because she lived before Christ. But we have no reason for ignorance; a clear choice is set before us. We can either occupy our days with the things of this world, which won't last, or give ourselves wholeheartedly to being part of the church—the bride of Christ.

We can best serve the purpose of God in our generation by becoming functioning members of a local expression of the body of Christ, making ourselves available to be used. Just a few are called to be leaders and prominent ministers. But all of us—children, young people, older ones, singles and

married couples—make up the family of God and
hold it together by our practical love and care for
one another.

I recently began sorting through a mass of old
photos I had accumulated, placing them in albums.
It took me a few months after Arthur's death to feel
prepared to stir so many memories, knowing they
would evoke a mixture of joy and pain. These
photos, some from the earliest days of our marriage
up until Arthur's death, formed a record of how we
served the purpose of God in our years together.
Events that once seemed so ordinary now take on a
new significance. Like pieces of a jigsaw puzzle,
they form a beautiful picture of God's purpose taking shape in our lives. Knowing that God will be
fitting the rest of the pieces from my life into the
picture of his purpose enables me to look forward
with hope to the future.

Some people who were writing articles about
Arthur's life and ministry asked me for a few photos
of some significant events. My albums are filled
with pictures of great value to me and my family,
but most of them would be meaningless to
strangers. I found only a few photos anybody might
think were 'significant'.

The Bible is a kind of photo album in which we
turn the pages and look at the men and women God
used to accomplish his plans. I wonder how many
people recorded in the Bible would really rate, in
our human estimation, as worthy of being there?
Isn't it amazing, for instance, that the writer of
Numbers or Chronicles did not skip over the long
list of descendants, as we do when we read them,
but instead mentions each one by name? God's plan

includes many obscure people the world would leave out. Though they might seem to us to have no particular significance, God has placed them in his photo album because he values each one highly and has used them to fulfil his purposes. One day we will understand more fully how they fit into his perfect plan.

At the next opportunity, take some time to look at the names that appear in the Bible and be encouraged as you observe who was worthy of being remembered in this way. Look beyond the obvious names like Solomon and David, Abraham and Sarah, Mary and Jesus' disciples. At the beginning of the year I began going through the Old Testament from the beginning, reading a few chapters a day. Only this morning I came across one of those lists of names, an account of Esau's sons. This time I read it carefully. I was intrigued to find the names of the 'grandsons of Esau's wife', and the mention made of a particular grand-daughter, sister, or wife. Were these women of influence? Women respected by their families and friends?

Consider Deborah, for example. Of course, we immediately think of the courageous prophetess who provoked the Israelites to rise up and resist their oppressors. But in this morning's Bible reading, I found another Deborah I had hardly noticed before. She was Rebekah's nurse. This woman accompanied Rebekah on her journey with Abraham's servant to become Isaac's wife. That's almost all we know about her. But by accompanying Rebekah, Deborah served the purpose God was to accomplish through the birth of Isaac, the son of promise. When Deborah died, the family named a

tree in her honour (Gen 35:8). Was she just a nanny?
No, the respect shown after her death indicates that
this Deborah was someone special.

I'd like to start collecting biblical references to
women like Deborah. There must be many of them.
Think of the midwives who risked their lives by
refusing to obey Pharaoh's command to kill every
newborn boy; Moses' mother, who made a floating
cradle for her precious son; the widow who put her
last coin in the offering, unaware that Jesus was
watching; Rhoda, a servant girl who answered the
door; Rufus's mother, who was like a mother to
Paul; and Dorcas, who was good at needlework.
Each one served the purpose of God in her generation.

There are many women today who are playing a
vital part in the church without fuss or the need for
a title—mothers, grandmothers, office workers,
ordinary people who are part of the family of God.
In a large church, to most of the congregation they
may be just names on an address list. But their
leaders probably know about them, and more
importantly, God does not forget their labours and
'the love you have shown him as you have helped
his people' (Heb 6:10).

I know many women who invest their time in the
Lord's work, doing such things as buying furniture
for poor people, visiting patients referred to them
by Christian doctors, counselling, praying for
people, making and selling crafts, joining in evangelistic outreaches, ushering, running a pregnancy
counselling centre, bringing people meals, writing
letters, providing housing and hospitality. The list
of opportunities to serve is endless. Two of the

oldest members of our church bless me most just by the effort they make to attend services and by joining in happily with younger people, who love to have them around.

These days, amid the controversy in some circles about female ordination and women in leadership, we can be in danger of missing the fact that God's purpose includes every woman, not just a gifted minority. We do not have to wait to be recognised, ordained, or given a title (which presumably only lasts until we are no longer physically fit to qualify), but we have a contribution to make as long as we live.

A friend of mine is now in her eighties. When she was twenty-five and single, she left home for India. There she was married and served the Lord for many years with her husband, enduring poor conditions and many hazards and hardships to proclaim the good news. We first met when they returned to England, where both of them continued to bring many to Christ. My friend was effective in ministering to both girls and older women and was much sought after as a speaker. But with four children of her own, life was full and she needed help in the home. A single woman felt God prompting her to help in my friend's home so she could continue her speaking ministry. I am sure this single woman shared the blessing of this woman's ministry and will one day have her reward at the judgement seat of Christ.

My friend's husband passed away, and for some years she has been increasingly disabled. The same single lady, also in her eighties now, has continued to be her companion and helper. Together they continue to serve the purpose of God. Losing her sight and no longer able to drive herself to meetings, my friend still seizes every opportunity to speak of her wonderful Saviour. She joined a club for the disabled, and her bright personality and radiant testimony brought joy and hope to its members. Now she has difficulty reading without a huge magnifying glass and very large print, so she has joined the Society for the Blind.

Undeterred by her limitations, this woman has found a new way to be used. Still possessing a beautiful singing voice, she records herself singing gospel songs, reading scriptures, and offering words of encouragement and testimony of how God has undertaken for her in the midst of her handicapped condition. These tapes then circulate among a handful of visually impaired people. Very few people know about this ministry. The Christian media hasn't done any news stories on it. Humanly speaking, this ministry is very limited compared with the many opportunities my friend had in her younger years. The tapes she makes are nothing professional. But I believe that this fruit, in its mellow maturity, is even more precious to God.

My friend and her companion are also women of prayer. In touch with the God of all creation from their home in a quiet country village, they wield as much power as the most prominent Christian leader. I visit their home occasionally and, like their other guests, always go away uplifted and with my vision of our heavenly Father enlarged. So at the end of their lives, in the midst of the physical limitations of age and disability, these women are exercising a valuable ministry.

Facing your future with hope

The pages of history for the remaining years of your life have yet to be written. As you face the future, be renewed with fresh hope. Determine to be among that great company of women who have served God right to the end of their lives. Have that last snapshot of yourself in the family photo album depict someone like Naomi, a woman still bearing fruit in her last years; a woman who is, indeed, worth following.

Bible Study: Considering what you've learned

1. Take time to think about what is the most significant lesson you have learned from the life of Naomi. If you're studying alone, write it in your notebook. If you're in a group, share the various lessons you've learned.

2. Write or discuss how you would like your life in the future to change because of what you've learned.

3. Is there a particular area of your life that you need to adjust in order to be 'worth following'? You may not feel free to share this with others, but if you do, pray for one another.

4. Read Hebrews 10:19–25. What do you find to encourage you in this passage? Be an encourager by telling someone what you appreciate about her and what aspects of her life are a good example for others to follow.

5. Romans 15:13 is a good verse to learn by heart. Read it aloud. If you're in a group, read it together, claiming it as a promise.